TRUTH

PLAIN AND SIMPLE

And Other Gospel Sermons

Andrew D. Erwin

Charleston, AR

COBB PUBLISHING

2018

Gospel Gleaner Publications
PO Box 456
Fayetteville, TN 37334
www.gospelgleaner.com
andyerwin@gospelgleaner.com

All Scripture references are taken from the New King James Version unless otherwise noted.

Published by
Cobb Publishing
704 E. Main St.
Charleston, AR 72933
(479) 747-8372
CobbPublishing@gmail.com
www.CobbPublishing.com

ISBN: 978-1-947622-09-8

In Memory

In one of her Bibles, I found this saying: "But we will have a better stay if we will bloom where we are planted." Indeed my maternal grandmother, Mary Belle Horner Bates, bloomed wherever she was planted – whether it was Perry County Tennessee, where she was born and raised; Hickman County Tennessee, where she labored as a wife, mother, and school teacher; or Weakley County Tennessee, where she spent her last twenty years of earthly life.

With all the thankfulness my heart can render, I am thankful to my eternal Father for allowing me the privilege to have her as my "Grandma Bates." It is in her memory that this book of sermons is lovingly dedicated. Truly, "To live in the hearts we leave behind is not to die."

In Loving Memory

Mary Belle Horner Bates
September 9, 1913- March 1, 2004

Grandma's Bible

My maternal grandmother was a guiding influence for New Testament Christianity in my family. As a child, her family helped to begin the Lord's church at Cedar Creek in Perry County, Tennessee. As an adult, she helped to convert her husband, daughter, son-in-law, and grandsons. She also helped to influence the children she taught for 33 years as an elementary educator in Hickman and Perry County, Tennessee.

Mary Belle Bates left this world for glory on March 1, 2004. Seeing that I was a young preacher, my mother saw fit to give me her biblical studies library, which included many commentaries, concordances, Bible dictionaries, and Bibles. She was a serious student of the word of God.

Her collection of Bibles was an interesting assortment of translations and study Bibles. She also had one Bible which she purchased from B.B. James, a favorite gospel preacher of our family, from his time as a Bible salesman. But, the centerpiece of this collection was her favorite and most used Bible at the time of her death.

Reflections about Her Bible

A person's Bible speaks volumes about his or her attitude toward the word of God.

Concerning this particular Bible, it is very telling to note that this was but one Bible in a long line of well-worn Bibles. In other words, these Bibles were used. I am reminded of the old song, "Dust on the Bible." Truly, there was no dust on this Bible!

The well-worn cover of this Bible is a testimony to her study habits. She read it often. She carried it with her. She carried it often. She took advantage of the opportunities she had to study the word of God.

Within this well-worn cover, you will find well-worn pages that are filled with marginal notes. Her notes reflect the depth and breadth of her studies. She wanted to remember verses and sermon notes on first principle matters, the church, Christian living, the Godhead, Bible translations, and key words within the text.

When a sermon was preached on a subject of particular interest, she would jot down the key points and even significant thoughts given by the preacher. For example:

"There is never a time to be un Christian."

"The person in love with self has no rival!!!"

"Live each day as though it were the last. Be prepared!"

"But we can have a happier stay if we bloom where we are planted."

Having reached 90 years of age, she also quoted Psalm 92:14: "They shall still bring forth fruit in old age; they shall be fat and flourishing."

The context from which this passage comes is quite comforting. "The righteous shall flourish like the palm tree: he shall grow like a cedar in Lebanon. Those that be planted in the house of the LORD shall flourish in the courts of our God. They shall still bring forth fruit in old age; they shall be fat and flourishing; To show that the LORD is upright: he is my rock, and there is no unrighteousness in him" (Psalm 92:12-15).

Grandma's Bible tells me that she was a student of the word of God. Her Bible tells me that she was a Christian. She understood the gospel plan of salvation and obeyed it. She was added to the Lord's church and understood that vital concept. She knew about Christian virtue, and the loveliness of Christian womanhood. She grew in the word, even

6

unto an advanced age. She was ever-learning, but unlike the women mentioned in 2 Timothy 3:7, she was able to come to know the truth. Indeed she brought forth fruit in old age.

Perhaps the most precious memory I have of this Bible, is the memory of my Grandma Bates sitting in her favorite chair with this Bible in her lap explaining the plan of salvation, the Lord's church, and the Lord's return to me. Precious memories! How they linger! How they ever flood my soul!

What Does My Bible Say about Me?

Holding her Bible in my hand, and knowing how much it means to me, I cannot help but consider my own Bible. What does my Bible say about me?

Is it well-worn from years of study? Have I understood the words which teach us how to become children of God? Have I made any notes pertaining to life and godliness?

If perhaps, someday my Bible should be handed down to one of my children, could they tell how much the Lord meant to me? Could they see that I loved to study His word? Would they cherish receiving my Bible because they knew how much it meant to me?

Andy Erwin

Acknowledgments

It is my hope that these few lessons will help to impress upon the reader the holiness of the Christian religion, God's sovereign will purposed in His church, and the relative simplicity with which such profound subjects can be learned.

I take no credit for originality in these lessons. Perish the thought! These lessons are merely building upon the foundation laid by Christ, furthered by His apostles, and faithfully honored by gospel preachers of the truest form until now. May every preacher "take heed how he builds on it" (1 Corinthians 3:10).

I am indebted to such faithful men who have encouraged me personally and professionally in my work, study, and life as a preacher. It is my hope and prayer that this effort will accomplish the greatest possible good for God and His glory.

Andrew D. Erwin
  Fayetteville, Tennessee

Sermons

All the words of my mouth are with righteousness;
nothing crooked or perverse is in them.
They are all plain to him who understands,
and right to those who find knowledge.

Proverbs 8:8-9

TRUTH: PLAIN AND SIMPLE

Upon hearing that his son, Guy, had decided to be a gospel preacher, the great evangelist S.F. Hester said to him, "Keep it simple, son. Souls are starving for the pure and simple gospel of Jesus Christ." That advice served my friend Guy Hester for more than sixty years in the pulpit and thousands of souls came to be saved through his efforts. I cannot help but appreciate the many fine elders, preachers, brothers, and sisters in Christ that have influenced this world for the better because they were first influenced by the pure and simple gospel of Jesus Christ. My life has been made better having come to know and to love such people, and I'm sure that you feel the same way.

The world *still* needs the pure and simple gospel of Christ, and the advice to "keep it simple" would serve preachers well today. Souls need the truth – plain and simple! The matter is too important to make it complicated. Our souls are made pure by obeying the truth (1 Peter 1:22). We are sanctified by the truth (John 17:17). The truth can set us free (John 8:32).

When the pure and simple gospel is preached, the power of God is demonstrated. Paul wrote, "For I am not ashamed of the gospel of Christ, for it is the power of God to salvation for everyone who believes, for the Jew first and also for the Greek. For in it the righteousness of God is revealed from faith to faith; as it is written, 'The just shall live by faith'" (Romans 1:16-17).

We must never be ashamed to teach and preach the truth. The Savior said, "For whoever is ashamed of Me and My words in this adulterous and sinful generation, of him the Son of Man also will be ashamed when He comes in the glory of His Father with the holy angels" (Mark 8:38).

Jesus was a preacher of the pure and simple gospel. The common man heard him gladly. Every preacher should endeavor to preach the plain and simple truth so that "your faith should not stand in the wisdom of men, but in the power of God" (1 Corinthians 2:5). "For the preaching of the cross is to them that perish foolishness; but unto us which are saved it is the power of God" (1 Corinthians 1:18). Paul urged Timothy to "preach the word" (2 Timothy 4:2). In leading others to live by faith there is no substitute for the word of God.

TRUTH IS ESSENTIAL TO LIVING BY FAITH

Let us preach the word plain and simple so that men might live by faith. "But without faith it is impossible to please Him, for he who comes to God must believe that He is, and that He is a rewarder of those who diligently seek Him" (Hebrews 11:6). Man cannot believe that God *is* and that God *rewards* except by preaching and teaching the gospel. Paul asks, "How then shall they call on Him in whom they have not believed? And how shall they believe in Him of whom they have not heard? And how shall they hear without a preacher?" (Romans 10:14) Paul continues, "So then faith comes by hearing, and hearing by the word of God" (Romans 10:17).

"The just shall live by faith." Faith is not a blind leap in the dark as some would claim. Faith is the sub-stance, or that which stands under, that which supports, our religion. It is the "substance of things hoped for and the evidence of things not seen" (Hebrews 11:3).

Faith, as it is derived from the word of God, is the basis for the Christian religion. The word of God is at the heart of everything that is truly Christian. If the word of God is not the basis for one's religion, it is a baseless religion.

2

Religion that is based upon personal feelings and opinions, rather than the word of God, can never be "of faith." A person may have a very strong opinion, but that is all he will have. Regardless how strong this opinion may be, it cannot save. Salvation is "through faith and that not of yourselves" (Ephesians 2:8). Man must have faith to be saved.

Faith is not the result of an answer to prayer; it is the result of hearing the gospel. How crucial then is the work of gospel preaching! Jesus has said, "Go into all the world and preach the gospel to every creature. He who believes and is baptized shall be saved; he that does not believe shall be condemned" (Mark 16:15). The preaching of the gospel will be met with acceptance or rejection; faith or disbelief. Nevertheless, we must preach the word. "Faith comes by hearing and hearing by the word of God."

TRUTH IS ESSENTIAL TO BUILDING UP THE CHURCH

We also need the truth preached plainly and simply when it comes to building up the church. We must not "lose heart" (2 Corinthians 4:1). We must not "grow weary" (Galatians 6:9). We must be "steadfast, immovable, always abounding in the work of the Lord, knowing that your labor is not in vain in the Lord" (1 Corinthians 15:58). Such an attitude takes tremendous faith!

To "edify" is to "build up." The church can be edified by "speaking the truth in love" (Ephesians 4:15-16). It is unthinkable to deny the place of God's truth in God's plan for the spiritual and numerical growth of His people. Concerning spiritual growth, we must "grow in the grace and knowledge of the Lord" (2 Peter 3:18). Concerning numerical growth, the word of God is the seed of the kingdom (Luke 8:11). The seed must be sown and watered – that is, the word must be preached – in order for God to provide the

3

increase (1 Corinthians 3:6, 7). The parable of the sower illustrates to us how the word must be spread abroad. The more seed we spread – that is, the more fervent we are in preaching the gospel – the more increase will come.

The church of Christ must never abandon the truth. The church is "the pillar and ground of the truth" (1 Timothy 3:15). It is in the eternal plan and purpose of God, that "the manifold wisdom of God might be made known by the church...according to the eternal purpose which He accomplished in Christ Jesus our Lord" (Ephesians 3:10-11).

We must never lose sight of the fact that our place in this world is to serve as God's educational institution – from the cradle to the grave. We must dedicate ourselves to keeping the mission of Christ alive. While many congregations are struggling with change agents and outright apostasy, we know that if the truth of God's word is upheld from generation to generation, the church will remain strong.

There are many ways to be wrong, but only one way to be right. And it has always been required of God's people to make that distinction clearly. Before her captivity in Babylon, unrighteous Judah was filled with a multitude of corrupt spiritual leaders which led to her demise as a kingdom. God's indictment was clear, "Her priests have violated my law, and have profaned mine holy things: they have put no difference between the holy and profane, neither have they showed difference between the unclean and the clean, and have hid their eyes from my sabbaths, and I am profaned among them" (Ezekiel 22:26, KJV).

Without making any distinction between right and wrong, the people of God in the Old Testament would eventually profane Him and hide their eyes from His law. The correlation between their actions and the religious world today is abundantly clear. Certain lines of comparison can also be

4

drawn between the actions of Judah and the actions of the Lord's church today. Have we been careful to distinguish the holy from the profane? Do our people know the difference between the doctrine of Christ and the doctrines of men? Do they know how to tell the difference?

The church of our Lord is as distinct as the doctrine she teaches. If no distinction exists between our doctrine and the doctrines of men, inevitably no distinction will exist between the churches of Christ and the churches of men. We will become just another denomination among denominations.

A great many distinctions of right and wrong must be stressed in the Lord's church today. Not only should we continue to teach and preach the distinctive plan of salvation, we must also continue to teach the distinctive nature of the Lord's church, and all the biblical beliefs which separate us from the world.

Fundamentals must be taught and understood. The basic facts and distinctive nature of the Christian religion must be stressed. Christians must come to understand the meaning of "one Lord, one faith, and one baptism" (Ephesians 4:4-6). Brethren must believe the faith was "once and for all delivered to the saints" and be willing to contend for its defense (Jude 3). Truly, "Whosoever transgresses (*goes beyond*), and does not abide (*does not stay*) in the doctrine of Christ, has not God" (2 John 9). If we have not God, we have no hope (Ephesians 2:12).

It is no trivial thing to go beyond the boundaries of the written word of God. Faith comes by hearing this word. Without faith it is impossible to please God, and overcome the world (1 John 5:4). Anything introduced into the Christian religion and imbibed by men that is not "of faith" is sin (Romans 14:23), carrying the penalty of spiritual death

5

(Romans 6:23). One reaches this point of spiritual death by attempting to chart his own course and direct his own steps (Jeremiah 10:23), rather than walk by faith (2 Corinthians 5:7). To walk by faith, we must walk according to the word of God, for this is how true faith is derived.

Such fundamentals of sound doctrine need to be taught and stressed in the Lord's church today. It is a matter of right and wrong. If one is not willing to teach the fundamentals of the faith, they are wrong, if for no other reason than for failing to distinguish the holy from the profane.

God has given everything we need pertaining to the life (*the physical*) and godliness (*the spiritual*). Let us take advantage of the blessing God has given us in His word, and use it to make the clear distinction between right and wrong. One cannot stay right, without learning what is wrong.

TRUTH IS ESSENTIAL TO STRENGTHENING THE HOME

We need the truth plain and simple when it comes to strengthening our families. The home is the oldest institution and second only in importance to the church. As goes the home, so goes society.

Our society is imploding under the influence of worldliness. Have you ever seen a family strengthened because they were covetous? Have you ever known of immorality to help a home? Such sins are great enemies to the family and many homes lay in ruin this very moment because of these things.

Now let me ask you, have you ever known of a family that has been made better because of the influence of the gospel? Surely you have. Have you ever seen a marriage last for fifty or sixty years because the couple lived by the "Golden Rule" or forgave 70x7? I imagine we each can name a few. We need to put Christ and His truth back in our homes – plain and simple. The best advice that could be given to any family for increased faithfulness and happiness is to build their home on Christ and His truth.

Let parents not be afraid to teach their children the difference between right and wrong. May they paint the picture just as black and white as truth demands! Husbands love your wives as Christ loves the church. Wives honor and respect your husbands as the heads of your respective families. Children obey your parents in the Lord. When we do these things, we build our homes on the Rock of Christ rather than Satan's sinking sand. When we do so, we provide our families with the foundation necessary to stand the tests of time and temptation.

The home is facing a terrible enemy in Satan, and he is doing all he can to destroy the family as God would have it.

Currently 30,000 liquor merchandisers in this country make over 30 billion dollars a year. Truth is never used to promote alcohol – politicians will lie to bring it into a community; commercials will lie in their advertising; users will lie to hide it from others. The truth is that alcohol is a poison which will kill a person, family, and community slowly – drink by drink. It will poison the body, the soul, the family, and the community in which it enters.

"Alcohol remains the number-one drug problem in the United States. Nearly 17 million adults in the U.S. are dependent on alcohol or have other alcohol-related problems, and about 88,000 people die from preventable alcohol-related causes. In teenagers, alcohol is the most commonly abused drug. Thirty-five percent of teens have had at least one drink by age 15. Even though it is illegal, about 8.7 million people 12 to 20 years of age have had a drink in the past month, and this age group accounted for 11%

of all alcohol consumed in the U.S. Among under-aged youth, alcohol is responsible for about 189,000 emergency-room visits and 4,300 deaths annually. Withdrawal, for those physically dependent on alcohol, is much more dangerous than withdrawal from heroin or other narcotic drugs." (emedicinehealth.com; retrieved 2016)

The sexual perversions of fornication, adultery, and homosexuality are destroying the home as well. There are 42 million abortions committed every year worldwide, 115,000 every day. In the US, there are almost 1.5 million a year – 3,700 every day. 52% of these abortions are done by woman younger than twenty-five. 20% of abortions are committed by teens.

75% of Americans have had sex by age twenty. 85% have had sex by age twenty-one. Teen pregnancy is two-times higher in US than any other country.

Concerning our children, twenty-five million juvenile arrests occur every year primarily because of theft, violence, and drugs. 50% of all violent crimes are committed by teenagers. Teen suicide is the third leading cause of teenage death, homicide is second. The fastest growing market for anti-depressants in this country is preschoolers. Many children are being born out of wedlock. There has been a 66% increase in illegitimate children since 1980.

Concerning marriage, divorce numbers are off the chart. 40-50% of all first-time marriages end in divorce. 60-67% of second-time marriages divorce. The third time is not a charm as 73-74% of third-time marriages divorce. We are told that is we will live together first, the marriage will stand. Studies have shown that 85% of marriages in which the couple lived together first end in divorce.

We must decide what kind of home we want to have. We must decide who is going to govern our home. We have been trying it the devil's way; now how about trying it God's way? God's truth sets forth these plain and simple principles:

Genesis 2:18: "And the Lord God said, 'It is not good that man should be alone; I will make him a helper comparable to him.'" Man needs a helper to share the good times and make it through the tough ones. Man needs a helper to serve God and go to heaven.

Genesis 2:24: "Therefore a man shall leave his father and mother and be joined to his wife, and they shall become one flesh."

Ephesians 5:24: "Therefore, just as the church is subject to Christ, so let the wives be to their own husbands in everything." Such a command does not degrade women. Far from it! Marriage is a relationship of mutual respect and love. Read the next verse.

Ephesians 5:25, 28: "Husbands, love your wives, just as Christ also loved the church and gave Himself for it... So husbands ought to love their own wives as their own bodies; he who loves his wife loves himself."

Proverbs 22:6: "Train up a child in the way he should go, and when he is old he will not depart from it."

Ephesians 6:4: "And you, fathers, do not provoke your children to wrath, but bring them up in the training and admonition of the Lord."

Ephesians 6:1: "Children, obey your parents in the Lord, for this is right."

A casual reading of these verses proves to us that God's plan for the home is far different from the plan our society is pushing for the home. Mark and observe those homes who have followed God's plan and also those who have followed the plan of a worldly society and ask yourself what type of family you desire.

TRUTH IS ESSENTIAL TO SAVING SOULS

We need the truth, plain and simple, when it comes to saving lost souls. No one can be saved apart from the truth which is in Jesus Christ. Jesus said, "I am the way, the truth, and the life. No one comes to the Father except through Me" (John 14:6). True faith involves believing the facts of the gospel, obeying the commands of the gospel, and inheriting the promises of the gospel. To disbelieve and disobey the gospel is to reject its blessings.

The Lord has said it is the truth that makes men free, for "If you continue in My word, then are you My disciples indeed; And you shall know the truth, and the truth shall make you free" (John 8:31-32).

Peter has taught us that our souls can be purified in "obeying the truth" (1 Peter 1:22-25). James instructs us, "Therefore lay aside all filthiness and overflow of wickedness, and receive with meekness the implanted word, which is able to save your souls" (James 1:21).

Two passages found in 2 Thessalonians should be connected in this part of our discussion. Paul wrote of the coming of Christ, as He would be "revealed from heaven with His mighty angels, in flaming fire taking vengeance on those who do not know God, and on those who do not obey the gospel of our Lord Jesus Christ. These shall be punished with everlasting destruction from the presence of the Lord and from the glory of His power..." (2 Thessalonians 1:7-9).

10

He also prophesied of the coming apostasy and the typified lawless one saying, "The coming of the lawless one is according to the working of Satan, with all power, signs, and lying wonders, and with all unrighteous deception among those who perish, because they did not receive the love of the truth, that they might be saved. And for this reason God will send them strong delusion, that they should believe the lie, that they all may be condemned who did not believe the truth but had pleasure in unrighteousness" (2 Thessalonians 2:9-12).

By connecting these two statements we learn that who do not love and obey the gospel, or believe a lie instead of the truth, will be condemned or punished with everlasting destruction. Truly, God has revealed unto us a stern and sober warning. Each one of us needs the truth, plain and simple, to save our own soul.

CONCLUSION

If we will allow God's word to penetrate our hearts and consciences, and instruct us in the way of truth, we shall come to know the hope and blessed promises enjoyed only by those who trust, obey, and keep His everlasting word. If we will obey God, He will deliver us from the power of darkness, and place us into the kingdom of His dear Son (Colossians 1:13).

God does not desire for anyone to be lost, but for all to be saved (2 Peter 3:9). He is commanding all men everywhere to repent (Acts 17:30). On Pentecost, lost souls who were pricked in their hearts through the preaching of the gospel cried out, "Men and brethren, what shall we do?" Peter said unto them, "Repent, and let every one of you be baptized in the name of Jesus Christ for the remission of sins; and you shall receive the gift of the Holy Spirit" (Acts 2:37-38).

11

Having been buried with Christ by baptism into His death, you will be raised a new creature to walk in newness of life (Romans 6:3-4).

BEYOND THE AZURE BLUE

The Psalmist wrote of the wonderful works of God saying, "We will not hide them from their children, Telling to the generation to come the praises of the Lord, And His strength and His wonderful works that He has done" (Psalm 78:4).

We need to have this kind of attitude today. Our children must know about the strength and the wonderful works of God. As parents, we need to teach them. As God's people, we should be teaching the generation to come and thus securing a bright future for the Lord's church. Every soul needs to know about God. Every soul needs to know that He loves us and longs to save us.

How wonderful God is and how wonderful His love is toward sinful man! The wonderful works of God have been ultimately demonstrated by the giving of the One who is called "Wonderful." Isaiah wrote of Christ saying, "His name will be called Wonderful, Counselor, Mighty God, Everlasting Father, Prince of Peace" (Isaiah 9:6).

Jesus Christ is the "Prince of Peace." Jesus came into the world so that we can have peace with God and know the love of God truly. "And we have known and believed the love that God has for us. God is love, and he who abides in love abides in God, and God in him" (1 John 4:16).

God dwells in every person that loves Him. His love for every soul has been supremely manifested and forever recorded in the words: "For God so loved the world that He gave His only begotten Son, that whoever believes in Him should not perish but have everlasting life."

That little word "so" is so very important. It is an adverb of manner. God *so* loves the world. In this way, God *so* loved the world that He sent His only Son to die on our behalf, for the sins that we committed. "For He made Him who knew no sin to be sin for us, that we might become the righteousness of God in Him" (2 Corinthians 5:21).

It ought to bring tears to our eyes to know that we caused Jesus to suffer and die that cruel death on the cross. My sins and your sins put Him there. We are the guilty ones!

Truly, the love God has for us is amazing. His grace is truly amazing. "For when we were still without strength, in due time Christ died for the ungodly. For scarcely for a righteous man will one die; yet perhaps for a good man someone would even dare to die. But God demonstrates His own love toward us, in that while we were still sinners, Christ died for us" (Romans 5:6-8).

God loves our souls. However, God hates our sins. God is not like us. He is righteous and holy and He hates every evil thing. If we are involved in doing something that is evil, His face will be turned from us. "For the eyes of the Lord are on the righteous, and his ears are open to their prayers; but the face of the Lord is against those who do evil" (1 Peter 3:12).

God will not tolerate even looking upon that which is evil. In Isaiah 59:1-4, we read: "Behold, the Lord's hand is not shortened, that it cannot save; nor His ear heavy, that it cannot hear. But your iniquities have separated you from your God; and your sins have hidden His face from you, so that He will not hear. For your hands are defiled with blood, and your fingers with iniquity; your lips have spoken lies, your tongue has muttered perversity. No one calls for justice, nor does any plead for truth. They trust in empty words and speak lies; they conceive evil and bring forth iniquity."

When we consider Almighty God, we must consider Him correctly. We must think right about God. Beyond the azure blue is the God of grace, love, holiness, and justice.

THE GOD OF GRACE

The world can increase in pride of self, wealth, knowledge, and even technology; but until it begins to think right about God, it can never be right with God. In order for the world (or the church for that matter) to think right about God, certain attributes of His need to be understood. Let us begin with that most wonderful attribute of grace. The grace of God sets the Christian religion apart from every other religion. No other religion has a cross in it. By the grace of God, Jesus Christ tasted death for every man (Hebrews 2:9).

Grace is a determining/controlling attribute of God. By God's unlimited power He could have destroyed every living creature from the face of the earth with the flood; but Noah found grace in the eyes of God (Genesis 6:8). God's justice was righteous in determining to destroy the cities of the plain; but His grace would have spared the wicked in these cities for the sake of ten righteous souls (Genesis 18:16-33). God's foreknowledge saw what sinful men would do to His Son, but His grace sent Him anyway. God's holiness is unapproachable by such filthy rags as we are; but His grace cleanses us and allows us to enter His presence with boldness (Hebrews 4:16). It is because of God's grace that we can take comfort in all His other attributes.

It is a great challenge to teach on the subject of the grace of God because of so many prevailing misunderstandings. For some, His grace may seem too good to be true. They believe they can never be forgiven for what they have done. For others, His grace may seem *too true to be good*. These would argue that they do not have to change their ways in order to be saved by grace. However, Paul writes, "What shall we say then? Shall we continue in sin that grace may abound? Certainly not! How shall we who died to sin live any longer in it?" (Romans 6:1-2)

It takes understanding the reality of God's truth to understand the nature of His grace. Knowledge of His goodness and His truth are required to arrive at the whole truth on the subject of grace.

There are two extreme ideas about God and His grace. One person says "I'll never be good enough." They have failed to account for grace. Another person says "What I am doing is good enough." They have failed to receive grace. A heart that is full of the grace of God will never be content to say "It's good enough for God."

The grace of God has appeared to all men. Note, "For the grace of God that brings salvation has appeared to all men, teaching us that, denying ungodliness and worldly lusts, we should live soberly, righteously, and godly in the present age" (Titus 2:11-12). Some have chosen to ignore the teaching of grace. But, when a person truly understands the grace of God, their heart will be filled with: Gratitude (G); Reverence (R); Adoration (A); Character (C); and Endurance (E).

God's grace establishes our hearts (Hebrews 13:9). We conduct ourselves by grace in the world (2 Corinthians 1:12). We stand in the true grace of God (1 Peter 5:12). A heart that has been established by grace will share that grace; and in sharing the grace of God, we will be showing the Father to the world.

Through grace, God offers. By grace, God save. With grace, God empowers. Concerning his weakness and thorn in his flesh, God said to Paul, "My grace is sufficient for thee, My strength is made perfect in weakness" (2 Corinthians 12:7-10).

16

THE GOD OF LOVE

Our God is also the God of love – supreme love, divine love. God is love (1 John 4:8, 16). God's love is demonstrated as a Father toward His children. Our heavenly Father provides physically, spiritually, and faithfully. Our heavenly Father protects for our comfort, our deliverance, and our safety.

We have a heavenly Father who is longsuffering. He is a Father who rewards. He is a Father who instructs. His love is told, demonstrated, and explained. Our heavenly Father corrects and He keeps His word.

While every one of us would prefer to think of God in terms of love, the same Bible which declares His love also declares His hate. God hates the way and the thoughts of the wicked (Proverbs 15:9, 26). God hates all forms of idolatry (Deuteronomy 12:31). God hates divorce (Malachi 2:16). Seven things are an abomination to Him – a proud look, a lying tongue, hands that shed innocent blood, a heart that devises wicked plans, feet that are swift in running to evil, a false witness who speaks lies, and one who sows discord among brethren (Provers 6:16-19).

Concerning Israel, God said, "I will love them no more" (Hosea 9:15). He said, "I hate, I despise your feast days" (Amos 5:21). Moreover, "Your new moons and your appointed feasts my soul hates" (Isaiah 1:14). These statements require some explanation. Israel had become hypocritical, unmerciful, and idolatrous. God could stand them no longer. There comes a point when God can stand sin no more! "For the perverse person is an abomination to the Lord" (Proverbs 3:32). "He who justifies the wicked, and he who condemns the just, both of them alike are an abomina-

17

tion to the Lord" (Proverbs 17:15). God hates all workers of iniquity (Psalm 5:5).

Thus, God's love is conditional. He has said, "I love those who love Me" (Proverbs 8:17). He loves the righteous (Psalm 146:8). He loves all who love His Son (John 14:21; 16:27).

As badly as God hates sin and those dedicated to the advancement of sinful causes, God's love is greater and has been demonstrated for all men in Christ Jesus. How can God hate sin so badly and yet send His only-begotten Son to die for sinners? The answer: God is love. God's grace is His primary/controlling attribute. Everything He offers is because of love.

God's love can be received and it can be rejected. When one rejects the love of God, a hardening of the heart ensues. But, when one receives the love of God, he becomes God-like, Christ-like, and Spirit-filled. He becomes a selfless servant to God and man. He becomes obedient to the will of God by exchanging his will for God's will. He becomes more patient and longsuffering with his fellow man. He becomes more faithful, noble, and dependable to the church. Such a person becomes contagious. His heart and life becomes a mirror to reflect God's love to the world.

The world must know that God loves them, but also that His love must be received. God loves us too much to reject Him. God's love is too precious not to receive it and welcome Him wholeheartedly.

THE GOD OF HOLINESS

While it is wonderful to contemplate on the grace and love of God, to stop there would be to leave the painting unfinished. God is also holy. The holiness of God is not something we can learn from experience. It must be learned from divine revelation. From beginning to end, the Bible declares the holiness of God.

Moses declared, "Who is like You, O LORD, among the gods? Who is like You, glorious in holiness, Fearful in praises, doing wonders?" (Exodus 15:11).

Joshua admonished the people by saying, "You cannot serve the Lord, for He is a holy God. He is a jealous God; He will not forgive your transgressions nor your sins. If you forsake the Lord and serve foreign gods, then He will turn and do you harm and consume you, after He has done you good" (Joshua 24:19).

Hannah praised, "No one is holy like the LORD, For there is none besides You, Nor is there any rock like our God" (1 Samuel 2:2).

On many occasions in the Psalms and the Prophets, God is called "the Holy One of Israel."

When we come to the New Testament, we find our Lord referring to the Father as "Holy Father."

In Isaiah and in Revelation we hear the angels lauding God as "Holy, holy, holy"; "Lord God of hosts"; and "Lord God almighty" (Isaiah 6:3; Revelation 4:8).

In the presence of such holiness Isaiah confessed, "Woe is me! for I am undone; because I am a man of unclean lips, and I dwell in the midst of a people of unclean lips: for mine eyes have seen the King, the LORD of hosts" (Isaiah 6:5).

God is pure and absolutely holy all the time. When we are in the presence of God in worship, in prayer, and in life we are in the presence of pure holiness. Indeed, "Be ye holy for I am holy" (Leviticus 11:44; 1 Peter 1:16). God's holiness is the pattern which every Christian must ascribe to follow and determine to emulate.

God's Holiness	Our Holiness
None like Him (Psalm 86:8-10)	None like us (1 Peter 2:5, 9; 2 Corinthians 6:14-18)
He is not tempted with evil (James 1:13)	We must resist evil temptations (James 4:7)
He does not tempt others with evil (James 1:13)	We must not tempt others with evil (Matthew 18:6)
No darkness at all (1 John 1:5)	We must have no fellowship with darkness (Ephesians 5:11); and walk not in darkness (1 John 1:6)
Cannot look upon evil (Habakkuk 1:13)	We must not look upon evil, support evil, or partake in evil things (1 Corinthians 15:33; Revelation 2:2; Jude 23)
Unchanging, true holiness (Amos 4:2; Ephesians 4:24)	We must become holy and remain holy (Revelation 22:11)
Innate to His nature (Leviticus 19:2)	Must become our nature (2 Corinthians 7:1)

As Christians, we must take our place as the temple of God. God is calling us to be holy and anyone who would try to undermine this must be withstood.

THE GOD OF JUSTICE

Beyond the azure blue, we also find God to be the God of justice. God administers true and impartial justice by the standard of His own righteous character. God's justice differs from man's justice. God will not acquit the wicked

20

(Nahum 1:3). God will not succumb to societal pressure in His judgements. God's judgments cannot be bought or bribed (Deuteronomy 10:17). God's judgments are not biased. God's judgments are never wrong.

God is completely just in His character. In fact, all His ways are just (Deuteronomy 32:4). He is the God of justice (Isaiah 30:18).

God is completely truthful. All of His works are truth (Daniel 4:37). All of His words are truth (Psalm 19:7-8). All of His judgments are truth (Psalm 19:9).

God is completely impartial. Anyone can be saved and anyone can be lost. Unto the household of Cornelius, Peter declared, "In truth I perceive that God shows no partiality. But in every nation whoever fears Him and works righteousness is accepted by Him" (Acts 10:34).

God has demonstrated His justice to man in at least three ways. God's justice is demonstrated in giving us free-will. God created us with the ability to choose whether or not to serve Him. Only in this type of creation is God glorified by genuine and sincere service. If God created one to do evil, and then condemned him for doing evil, God would be unjust for condemning that person for doing what He created him to do.

Secondly, God's justice is also demonstrated in the principle of sowing and reaping. We reap what we sow. If we sow righteousness, we shall reap righteousness; if we sow wickedness, we shall reap wickedness (Galatians 6:7-10). If we sow bountifully, we will reap bountifully; if we sow sparingly, we shall reap sparingly (2 Corinthians 9:6). God is just in rewarding man according to his work (Revelation 20:12).

Thirdly, His justice will ultimately be demonstrated in the finality of His word. The false doctrine of Universalism

21

teaches that God will change His mind and save everyone. The Bible teaches that His word endures forever (Matthew 24:35; 1 Peter 1:22-25; Hebrews 2:1-4) and only those who obey Him will be saved (Hebrews 5:9). The Bible will read exactly the same on the Day of Judgment as it reads today.

CONCLUSION

The four attributes we have chosen to study are inseparable. God is just to punish because He is holy. God is willing to forgive because of His grace. God will have grace toward sinners because He is love. Let us determine to think right about God and present Him accurately to the world.

Beyond the azure blue, you will find the wonderful, loving, and all-powerful God. Beyond the azure blue, there is the God that created the heavens, the earth, the sea, and all things therein. "The heavens declare the glory of God; and the firmament shows His handiwork" (Psalm 19:1).

Beyond the azure blue, the God of forgiveness is not only willing to forgive you of your sins, but He is willing to blot them forever from His book of remembrance. God not only has the power to forgive, He also possesses the power to forget. He is promising to remember our sins no more (Hebrews 10:17). Beloved, this is a promise too good to refuse. Paul wrote to Titus about "our great God and Savior Jesus Christ, who gave Himself for us, that He might redeem us from every lawless deed and purify for Himself His own special people, zealous for good works" (Titus 2:14).

If you are seeking redemption, you must come to terms with the sacrifice of Jesus Christ. "In Him we have redemption through His blood, the forgiveness of sins, according to the richness of His grace" (Ephesians 1:7). We trust in these promises because we know that beyond the azure blue there

22

is the God that rewards. God is willing to reward any soul that will diligently seek Him. God *is* and God *rewards*.

Soon we shall stand before the holy God who created the heavens and the earth and demands to be obeyed, "And there is no creature hidden from His sight, but all things are naked and open to the eyes of Him to Whom we must give account" (Hebrews 4:13).

Beyond the azure blue, God is waiting to welcome our souls. Mercy and pardon flow fully and freely from His divine stream of redeeming love. Let us come to be blessed by the Giver of every good and perfect gift.

THE NATION OF ISRAEL
IN GOD'S SCHEME OF REDEMPTION

In Genesis 3:14-15, we read the first Messianic prophecy in the Bible. God was speaking to Satan, as follows: "So the Lord God said to the serpent: 'Because you have done this, you are cursed more than all cattle, and more than every beast of the field; on your belly you shall go, and you shall eat dust all the days of your life. And I will put enmity between you and the woman, and between your seed and her Seed; He shall bruise your head, and you shall bruise His heel.'"

You will observe that from the Seed of woman a Man would be born who would deliver a crushing death blow to the head of Satan. The Man foretold in this prophecy is the very same that is foretold in Isaiah's prophecy: "Therefore the Lord Himself will give you a sign: Behold, the virgin shall conceive and bear a Son, and shall call His name Immanuel" (Isaiah 7:14). Combine these two passages and you will find one is an extension of the other. Christ would come from the seed of woman *only*. Thus, it would naturally follow that His birth would have to be a virgin birth.

In Matthew's gospel record, the meaning of this prophecy is forever fixed by the inspired account of the angel's explanation to Joseph. The angel said, "Joseph, son of David, do not be afraid to take to you Mary your wife, for that which is conceived in her is of the Holy Spirit. And she will bring forth a Son, and you shall call His name Jesus, for He will save His people from their sins" (Matthew 1:20-21). Through Christ, God's people would be saved from their sins, securing their victory over Satan.

Matthew explains, "Now all this was done *that it might be fulfilled* which was spoken by the Lord through the prophet, saying: 'Behold, a virgin shall be with child, and bear a Son, and they shall call His name Immanuel,' which is translated, 'God with us'" (Matthew 1:22-23).

God would be with His people in the person of His Son, saving them from their sins. What would prove to be Satan's death has provided life for us. Paul wrote, "Much more then, having now been justified by His blood, we shall be saved from wrath through Him. For if when we were enemies we were reconciled to God through the death of His Son, much more, having been reconciled, we shall be saved by His life" (Romans 5:9-10).

Christ came to save His people from the wrath of sin and also from the sting of death. To do this, He would have to destroy Satan. Hebrews 2:14-15 reads, "Inasmuch then as the children have partaken of flesh and blood, He Himself likewise shared in the same, that through death He might destroy him who had the power of death, that is, the devil, and release those who through fear of death were all their lifetime subject to bondage."

The strength of sin and death would forever be removed for those who are sanctified by the offering of Jesus Christ. "For by one offering He has perfected forever those who are being sanctified" (Hebrews 10:14).

It was not God's will that Christ be offered many times, or on a regular basis, as in the annual Day of Atonement, but once in these last days, the last dispensation of the world's history.

"For Christ has not entered the holy places made with hands, which are copies of the true, but into heaven itself, now to appear in the presence of God for us; not that He should offer Himself often, as the high priest enters the Most

26

Holy Place every year with blood of another He then would have had to suffer often since the foundation of the world; but now, once at the end of the ages, He has appeared to put away sin by the sacrifice of Himself" (Hebrews 9:24-26).

None of this happened by chance. It was all according to God's supreme strategy to defeat Satan, the adversary of man, and to bless all nations with the opportunity of fellowship and salvation with Him. God would bring His Son into the world. As we have previously noted, God's Son was going to be born of a virgin, of the seed of woman. But, from whence would this woman come? Answering this question will introduce us to the family of Abraham and the children of Israel.

THE PLACE OF ABRAHAM

God selected one man and one seed to bring forth His Son. The man He selected was Abram or Abraham (Genesis 12). It would be from this one man's seed or nation of descendants that all the nations of the earth would be blessed. God promised to Abraham, "I will bless those who bless you, and I will curse him who curses you; and in you all the families of the earth shall be blessed" (Genesis 12:3).

From this promise we can learn that it was never God's intention to value one nation over others, but by one nation, or family, all nations, or families, would be blessed. By inspiration, Paul assures us that this promise unto all nations is now accomplished by faith in Christ. "For you are all sons of God through faith in Christ Jesus. For as many of you as were baptized into Christ have put on Christ. There is neither Jew nor Greek, there is neither slave nor free, there is neither male nor female; for you are all one in Christ Jesus. And if you are Christ's, then you are Abraham's seed, and heirs according to the promise" (Galatians 3:26-29).

27

A careful study of Galatians chapter three would be most beneficial to the student of this subject. Therein, Paul teaches us to "know that only those who are of faith are sons of Abraham" (Galatians 3:7).

He continues by commenting on the promise made to Abraham, "And the Scripture, foreseeing that God would justify the nations by faith, preached the gospel to Abraham beforehand, saying, 'In you all the nations shall be blessed.' So then those who are of faith are blessed with believing Abraham" (Galatians 3:8-9).

Upon these facts Paul concludes, "For you are all sons of God through faith in Christ Jesus...And if you are Christ's, then you are Abraham's seed, and heirs according to the promise" (Galatians 3:26 and 29).

THE PLACE OF CIRCUMCISION AND THE SABBATH

Two signs given unto the Jews pertaining to this promise should be discussed. First, circumcision was given as a sign of the covenant God made with Abraham. It was an exclusive sign for an exclusive covenant. The fact that circumcision has absolutely no spiritual significance today should prove to us that this covenant has been fulfilled and all nations can be blessed by Christ.

Observe, "For in Christ Jesus neither circumcision nor uncircumcision avails anything, but faith working through love" (Galatians 5:6).

Again, "For in Christ Jesus neither circumcision nor uncircumcision avails anything, but a new creation" (Galatians 6:15).

Circumcision is no longer a commandment of God. Note, "Was anyone called while circumcised? Let him not become uncircumcised. Was anyone called while uncircumcised? Let him not be circumcised. Circumcision is nothing

28

and uncircumcision is nothing, but keeping the commandments of God is what matters" (1 Corinthians 7:18-19).

The Law of Moses was added in the same way. It was an exclusive law for an exclusive nation. Israel was the only nation ever intended to be governed by that law. It was added to Israel because of Israel's transgressions, to serve as a schoolmaster, or tutor, to bring Israel to faith in Christ.

Note: "What purpose then does the law serve? It was added because of transgressions, till the Seed should come to whom the promise was made; and it was appointed through angels by the hand of a mediator. Now a mediator does not mediate for one only, but God is one. Is the law then against the promises of God? Certainly not! For if there had been a law given which could have given life, truly righteousness would have been by the law. But the Scripture has confined all under sin, that the promise by faith in Jesus Christ might be given to those who believe. But before faith came, we were kept under guard by the law, kept for the faith which would afterward be revealed. Therefore the law was our tutor to bring us to Christ, that we might be justified by faith. But after faith has come, we are no longer under a tutor" (Galatians 3:19-25).

The second sign of God's covenant with Abraham is the Sabbath, which also served as a sign of this law for this one nation.

Read with me beginning at Exodus 31:12, "And the Lord spoke to Moses, saying, 'Speak also to the children of Israel, saying: `Surely My Sabbaths you shall keep, for it is a sign between Me and you throughout your generations, that you may know that I am the Lord Who sanctifies you. You shall keep the Sabbath, therefore, for it is holy to you. Everyone who profanes it shall surely be put to death; for whoever does any work on it, that person shall be cut off from among his people. Work shall be done for six days, but the seventh is the Sabbath of rest, holy to the Lord. Whoever does any work on the Sabbath day, he shall surely be put to death. Therefore the children of Israel shall keep the Sabbath, to observe the Sabbath throughout their generations as a perpetual covenant. It is a sign between Me and the children of Israel forever; for in six days the Lord made the heavens and the earth, and on the seventh day He rested and was refreshed.' And when He had made an end of speaking with him on Mount Sinai, He gave Moses two tablets of the Testimony, tablets of stone, written with the finger of God."

The sign of the Sabbath was to exist between God and Israel. It was also to be observed throughout their generations, which gives us some insight into the idea of "forever" or "perpetual." The Hebrew word translated "forever" or "perpetual"– *olam* – can mean everlasting in the sense of eternal, and it can also mean "for the distant future." Such was also the use of this word pertaining to the Levitical priesthood in Exodus 29:9. Like the priesthood of Aaron, the Sabbath was to be a perpetual statute as long as that law lasted.

In the case of the Sabbath, the Bible tells us that it lasted as long as it was intended to last. Paul warns Christians to let no man judge them with regards to keeping laws pertaining to meat, drink, holydays, new moons, or Sabbath days (Colossians 2:16). He said that such was, "a shadow of things to come, but the substance is of Christ" (Colossians 2:17). All of which has been nailed to His cross (Colossians 2:14).

THE PLACE OF THE CROSS IN FULFILLING THE LAW

Christ was offered on the cross, becoming accursed, so that He might take away the curse of the law from Israel (cf.

Deuteronomy 21:22; Galatians 3:12). He nailed the law to His cross. The veil of the law is done away in Christ (2 Corinthians 3:14).

He did not take some of the law or most of the law out of the way, but every precept in the Law of Moses was fulfilled in Christ (Matthew 5:17-18). He inaugurated for us a new and living way (Hebrews 10:20). He made this first covenant old by His death on the cross (Hebrews 8:13) and replaced it with a better covenant (Hebrews 8:6). By so doing, He took the enmity, which was the law, away from Jews and Gentiles making one new man and one new nation of every nation on earth.

Read carefully with me from Ephesians 2:11-22, "Therefore remember that you, once Gentiles in the flesh who are called Uncircumcision by what is called the Circumcision made in the flesh by hands that at that time you were without Christ, being aliens from the commonwealth of Israel and strangers from the covenants of promise, having no hope and without God in the world. But now in Christ Jesus you who once were far off have been made near by the blood of Christ. For He Himself is our peace, Who has made both one, and has broken down the middle wall of division between us, having abolished in His flesh the enmity, that is, the law of commandments contained in ordinances, so as to create in Himself one new man from the two, thus making peace, and that He might reconcile them both to God in one body through the cross, thereby putting to death the enmity. And He came and preached peace to you who were afar off and to those who were near. For through Him we both have access by one Spirit to the Father. Now, therefore, you are no longer strangers and foreigners, but fellow citizens with the saints and members of the household of God, having been built on the foundation of the apostles and prophets,

Jesus Christ Himself being the chief cornerstone, in whom the whole building, being joined together, grows into a holy temple in the Lord, in Whom you also are being built together for a habitation of God in the Spirit."

Gentiles are now members of the household of God, not on the basis of the law which was abolished, but on the basis of being reconciled to God by the blood of Christ Jesus. Granted, many of the moral commandments of the law can be found in Christ's new covenant, but they are binding upon the faithful of every nation because *His* covenant is for every nation, not because we are commanded to obey the law given to Israel. We ought not to consider it to be a strange thing that God's sense of morality did not change from a covenant for one nation unto a covenant for every nation. God's sense of morality is forever the same.

THE PLACE OF THE CHURCH AS THE KINGDOM OF GOD

Some will say that Israel remains God's chosen people today. However, Peter gave this designation to the church. "But you are a chosen generation, a royal priesthood, a holy nation, His own special people, that you may proclaim the praises of Him who called you out of darkness into His marvelous light; who once were not a people but are now the people of God, who had not obtained mercy but now have obtained mercy" (1 Peter 2:9-10).

Paul spoke the same message essentially in Ephesians chapter three. Read with me how "that the Gentiles should be fellow heirs, of the same body, and partakers of His promise in Christ through the gospel" (Ephesians 3:6).

Also read how that Paul was to preach "among the Gentiles the unsearchable riches of Christ, and to make all people see what is the fellowship of the mystery, which from the beginning of the ages has been hidden in God who created all things through Jesus Christ; to the intent that now the manifold wisdom of God might be made known by the church to the principalities and powers in the heavenly places, according to the eternal purpose which He accomplished in Christ Jesus our Lord, in whom we have boldness and access with confidence through faith in Him" (Ephesians 3:8-12).

It is the church, not the nation of Israel, that is the fullness of Christ (Ephesians 1:23). Every spiritual blessing is in Christ, not in the nation of Israel (Ephesians 1:3). In fact, the church is now designated as the "Israel of God" (Galatians 6:16).

THE PLACE OF THE NATION OF ISRAEL IN THE SCHEME OF REDEMPTION HAS BEEN FULFILLED

Having collected and analyzed all of these various ideas, we come to the conclusion that God fulfilled everything He intended to accomplish with the seed of Abraham when Christ was brought forth of a virgin. Holy Scripture bears this out. All nations of the earth are now blessed by Christ. The gospel is to be preached to all nations (Luke 24:47), unto the uttermost parts of the world (Acts 1:8), and to all who are afar off, "as many as the Lord our God shall call" (Acts 2:39).

The Old Testament prophets pointed to the day of Christ with unanimity. Moses spoke of the Prophet, the Christ, who would come and said, "Unto to Him shall ye hearken." Jeremiah wrote of the new covenant God would make with the house of Israel and the house of Judah (Jeremiah 31:31-33). And, Isaiah tells of a new name that would be given to God's people after the family was enlarged to include the Gentiles (Isaiah 62:1-2).

Quoting from Jeremiah, the writer of Hebrews observes, "For if that first covenant had been faultless, then no place would have been sought for a second. Because finding fault with them, He says: 'Behold, the days are coming,' says the Lord, 'when I will make a new covenant with the house of Israel and with the house of Judah not according to the covenant that I made with their fathers in the day when I took them by the hand to lead them out of the land of Egypt; because they did not continue in My covenant, and I disregarded them,' says the Lord" (Hebrews 8:7-9).

Peter preached, "Yes, and all the prophets, from Samuel and those who follow, as many as have spoken, have also foretold these days. You are sons of the prophets, and of the covenant which God made with our fathers, saying to Abraham, 'And in your seed all the families of the earth shall be blessed'" (Acts 3:24-25).

Christ declared of Himself, "These are the words which I spoke to you while I was still with you, that all things must be fulfilled which were written in the Law of Moses and the Prophets and the Psalms concerning Me" (Luke 24:44).

The prophets spoke what was for them a mystery or hidden thing (1 Peter 1:10-12; Ephesians 3:2-6). God's strategy was not unfolded or revealed until the fullness of times (Ephesians 1:10). We now live in the fullness of times, the last days.

"God, who at various times and in different ways spoke in time past to the fathers by the prophets, has in these last days spoken to us by His Son, whom He has appointed heir of all things, through Whom also He made the world" (Hebrews 1:1-2).

For any man to be saved today, whether Jew or Greek, he must be saved by the gospel. According to Paul, the gospel of Christ is "the power of God to salvation for everyone who believes, for the Jew first and also for the Greek. For in it the righteousness of God is revealed from faith to faith; as it is written, 'The just shall live by faith'" (Romans 1:16-17).

All men are saved by the same blessed covenant and terms. Speaking of Gentiles and Jews Peter said, "But we believe that through the grace of the Lord Jesus Christ we shall be saved in the same manner as they" (Acts 15:11).

Paul preached, "Truly, these times of ignorance God overlooked, but now commands all men everywhere to repent, because He has appointed a day on which He will judge the world in righteousness by the Man Whom He has ordained. He has given assurance of this to all by raising Him from the dead" (Acts 17:30-31), and "that no flesh should glory in His presence" (1 Corinthians 1:29), for "there is no partiality with God" (Romans 2:11).

The kingdom of God was preached to Jews (Acts 28:23), Samaritans (Acts 8:12), and Gentiles (Acts 19:8; Acts 20:25; Acts 28:31). Paul testified to Jews and Greeks the same message of repentance toward God and faith toward the Lord Jesus Christ (Acts 20:21). The great apostle's desire was for Israel to be saved, but he also understood such salvation would only come through the gospel.

Paul wrote, "Brethren, my heart's desire and prayer to God for Israel is that they may be saved. For I bear them witness that they have a zeal for God, but not according to knowledge. For they being ignorant of God's righteousness, and seeking to establish their own righteousness, have not submitted to the righteousness of God. For Christ is the end of the law for righteousness to everyone who believes" (Romans 10:1-4).

Paul understood God would grant, "eternal life to those who by patient continuance in doing good seek for glory, honor, and immortality; but to those who are self-seeking and do not obey the truth, but obey unrighteousness indignation and wrath, tribulation and anguish, on every soul of man who does evil, of the Jew first and also of the Greek; but glory, honor, and peace to everyone who works what is good, to the Jew first and also to the Greek. For there is no partiality with God" (Romans 2:7-11).

To the Jews of Paul's day, this was not a satisfactory saying. They were trying to establish their own righteousness apart from righteousness through faith. As long as they were so doing, they would be ignorant of God's righteousness and outside of the shelter of salvation.

For a person to say the Jews are saved one way and the Gentiles another would be contrary to all these scriptures. As Christians, our mission is to preach the gospel to every creature (Mark 16:15) in every nation (Matthew 28:19). Every man is subject to the authority of Christ and must obey all His commandments – whether we are Jews or Gentiles. We must follow Christ (1 Corinthians 11:1; Philippians 3:16-17).

CONCLUSION

The nation of Israel served a unique purpose in God's eternal plan. Abraham is truly the father of the faithful (James 2:21). Through his seed our precious and dear Savior was born. God's covenant with Abraham was for an intended purpose to last for an intended time. God's intentions have been revealed, realized, and received.

Let us rejoice in faith and in the new birth which adds us to God's all-encompassing family of every nation, kindred, people, and tongue (Revelation 7:9). You can become a child of God today, but you must be born into His family. This birth is not of flesh and blood, but of water and Spirit. Jesus said, "That which is born of the flesh is flesh, and that which is born of the Spirit is spirit" (John 3:6). Man must be born again (John 3:7).

If you are going to be saved, you cannot trust in your physical birth. Salvation is not a birth right granted to certain families. God does not save nations. He saves individuals.

As an individual who will stand alone before Christ on the Judgment Day, you must make a personal decision today as to what you will do with Jesus. What will your answer be?

THE AUTHORITY AND TRUSTWORTHINESS OF THE BIBLE

Our theme for this lesson is: "The Authority and Trustworthiness of the Bible." Let us begin our study by defining the key terms of *authority* and *trustworthiness*.

When we speak of the *authority* of the Bible, we are speaking of the *governing, legislating, judging,* and *commanding power* of the Bible. In Matthew's account of the Great Commission, *exousia* is translated *power* in the King James Version, while it is translated *authority* in the New King James Version of the Bible (Matthew 28:18). Both are good translations of the word as Christ's *power* and His *authority* are synonymous terms when it comes to His governing rule. Christ does not have some authority, but *all* authority in matters of His church. "And He is the head of the body, the church, who is the beginning, the firstborn from the dead, that in *all* things He may have the preeminence" (Colossians 1:18).

The Bible has its authority because God has authority. To speak of the authority of the Bible is to speak of the authority of God. God has communicated His authority – His *power* in governing, legislating, judging, and commanding – in words which we can understand and know for certain. God governs His people completely. If it is your desire to be a child of God, then you are stating that it is your desire to submit to the will of God in every way.

Likewise, to speak of the trustworthiness of the Bible, is to speak of the trustworthiness of God. The Bible reveals that God is faithful and true, reliable and unchanging. If God is all these things (and He is) His word which bears witness of Him must likewise be faithful and true, reliable and unchanging; in other words, *trustworthy*. If a person will not accept the Bible to be authoritative and trustworthy in *every* way, he cannot accept the Bible as being authoritative and trustworthy in *any* way.

If we believe God, we will believe His word. We ought to believe the Bible to be reliable because God is reliable. God has proven His reliability to man in both word and deed. He has kept His word and done exactly as He has said He would on every occasion. Examples of God's prophecies and promises are found from Genesis to Revelation. All the prophets from Samuel onward have foretold of these last days (Acts 3:24). In fact, every Bible prophecy has been fulfilled with the exception of those pertaining to our Lord's return. Beloved, what does that say for the certainty of that event?

The Bible is trustworthy because it has honored and continues to honor its purpose in every way. In the long ago, the Lord swore to His prophet Isaiah saying: "For as the rain comes down, and the snow from heaven, And do not return there, But water the earth, And make it bring forth and bud, That it may give seed to the sower And bread to the eater, So shall My word be that goes forth from My mouth; It shall not return to Me void, But it shall accomplish what I please, And it shall prosper in the thing for which I sent it" (Isaiah 55:10-11).

HIS WORD HAS ALL-AUTHORITY

God has purposed to reveal Himself to us through His word. He has done this. His nature and character are revealed in the Bible. His righteousness and mercy are clearly seen. Without the Bible, we would know nothing of His grace or His will for our lives. At least two thousand times the Bible contains the phrase, "Thus says the Lord" or the equivalent thereof.

God has purposed to teach us of our origin, duty, and destiny. He has done this. We have no excuse to be ignorant of these things, for God has revealed them to us. The word is given so that we might grow in His grace and knowledge (2 Peter 3:18), not by twisting the truth (2 Peter 3:16), but by rightly dividing God's word in our studies and applications (2 Timothy 2:15).

We have the Bible to guide us throughout life. We are not to direct our own steps (Jeremiah 10:23), but live by the faith and righteousness revealed in the gospel (Romans 1:16-17). God sent His word into this world to serve as the sanctifying truth for whosoever would obey. Christ prayed, "Sanctify them by thy truth. Thy word is truth" (John 17:17). Everyone who is of the truth listens to Him (John 18:37).

Every word has been recorded by the authority of God. Every word is important. Ultimately, it is this word that shall serve as the standard for our judgment on the last day (John 12:48). Man should be found living by "every word that proceeds from the mouth of God" (Matthew 4:4).

Even the smallest markings of His word are important as Christ said: "Do not think that I came to destroy the Law or the Prophets. I did not come to destroy but to fulfill. For assuredly, I say to you, till heaven and earth pass away, one jot or one tittle will by no means pass from the law till all is fulfilled. Whoever therefore breaks one of the least of these commandments, and teaches men so, shall be called least in the kingdom of heaven; but whoever does and teaches them, he shall be called great in the kingdom of heaven" (Matthew 5:17-18).

Every word and each commandment has a purpose. Joshua was instructed to keep all the commandments of the Law in his conquest of Canaan. In the instructions given to

Joshua, God said: "Only be strong and very courageous, that you may observe to do according to all the law which Moses My servant commanded you; do not turn from it to the right hand or to the left, that you may prosper wherever you go. This Book of the Law shall not depart from your mouth, but you shall meditate in it day and night, that you may observe to do according to all that is written in it. For then you will make your way prosperous, and then you will have good success. Have I not commanded you? Be strong and of good courage; do not be afraid, nor be dismayed, for the LORD your God is with you wherever you go" (Joshua 1:7-9).

God's word to Joshua bore complete authority and he was to keep all of the commandments under the Law of Moses. If God required Israel to be obedient to the Law of Moses, surely He would require that Christians should be obedient to the Law of Christ. Indeed we are, as Christ has said: "All authority has been given to Me in heaven and on earth. Go therefore and make disciples of all the nations, baptizing them in the name of the Father and of the Son and of the Holy Spirit, teaching them to observe all things that I have commanded you; and lo, I am with you always, even to the end of the age" (Matthew 28:18-20).

Friends, this is not legalism. This is the inspired word of God. God's word is to be obeyed. And every word of God has its purpose.

Moreover, we are not to go beyond what is written in our estimation of men or their teachings (1 Corinthians 4:6). As a matter of fact, God views the Christian's fellowship with false teachers to be so serious, that He inspired John to write, "Whoever transgresses and does not abide in the doctrine of Christ does not have God. He who abides in the doctrine of Christ has both the Father and the Son. If anyone comes to you and does not bring this doctrine, do not receive him into your house nor greet him; for he who greets him shares in his evil deeds" (2 John 9-11).

"And no wonder! For Satan himself transforms himself into an angel of light. Therefore *it is* no great thing if his ministers also transform themselves into ministers of righteousness, whose end will be according to their works" (2 Corinthians 11:14-15).

Beloved, no man, no church, and no government, has the authority to bind upon you anything which God has not bound in divine service and worship to Him.   No man, council, congregation, or creed has ever had the authority to usurp, supplement or substitute the authority Christ has over His church —in any way — though many have tried.

Thus, the church must be true to the authority of Christ in all things (see Ephesians 1:22 and Colossians 1:18). Christ has all authority in His church, and by His authority we have our only creed – the New Testament.

Not even an angel from heaven has the authority to add to or to take from the gospel. The Galatians were warned that if any teacher sought to teach a gospel different than the gospel Paul and his companions had preached, and that they had received, that false teacher was to be accursed (Galatians 1:6-9).

HIS WORD IS ALL-SUFFICIENT

The Bible is not only all-authoritative; it is also all-sufficient. Through knowledge of the Son of God we have "all things pertaining to life and godliness" (2 Peter 1:3-4). If it is not in the Bible, it does not pertain to life and godliness.

The Holy Spirit guided the apostles into "all truth" (John 16:13). If it is not in the Bible, it is not truth. Where in the

Bible to we read of the many modern theological doctrines and denominations? Where do we find cult groups such as Mormons or Jehovah's Witnesses? Where to we find their "sacred" writings? The Holy Spirit guided the apostles into all truth. If the apostles did not write about it, then it did not come from God.

"All Scripture is given by inspiration of God, and is profitable for doctrine, for reproof, for correction, for instruction in righteousness, that the man of God may be complete, thoroughly equipped for every good work" (2 Timothy 3:16-17). Within the Bible, a person can find the answers to the questions of what must I do to be saved, and what must I do to remain saved? One can learn about the church of Christ. One can learn about worshipping in spirit and truth. Truly, the man of God can be equipped for every good work.

Just how were the apostles inspired to write what would become the New Testament scriptures? Listen carefully: "But God has revealed them to us through His Spirit. For the Spirit searches all things, yes, the deep things of God. For what man knows the things of a man except the spirit of the man which is in him? Even so no one knows the things of God except the Spirit of God. Now we have received, not the spirit of the world, but the Spirit who is from God, that we might know the things that have been freely given to us by God. These things we also speak, not in words which man's wisdom teaches but which the Holy Spirit teaches, comparing spiritual things with spiritual" (1 Corinthians 2:10-13).

Also, carefully read 2 Peter 1:19-21: "And so we have the prophetic word confirmed, which you do well to heed as a light that shines in a dark place, until the day dawns and the morning star rises in your hearts; knowing this first, that no prophecy of Scripture is of any private interpretation, for prophecy never came by the will of man, but holy men of God spoke as they were moved by the Holy Spirit."

The word of God was revealed to men of God by the Spirit of God. Why? Paul said, "So that we might know the things that have been freely given to us by God." How? Peter said not "of any private interpretation, for prophecy never came by the will of man, but holy men of God spoke as they were moved by the Holy Spirit."

HIS WORD IS TRUSTWORTHY

God wants us to know Him truly. In order for us to know God truly, He has given us a true word whereby to learn of Him. His word is true, reliable, and infallible. "The judgments of the Lord are true and righteous altogether" (Psalm 19:9). "Thy word is truth" (John 17:17).

God desires that we have a true conception of Him and that our faith in Him is based upon His truth. Faith is trusting that God has told you the truth and that His word is correct. Faith means believing "In hope of eternal life, which God, that cannot lie, promised before the world began..." (Titus 1:2). Therefore, because "it was impossible for God to lie, we might have a strong consolation, who have fled for refuge to lay hold upon the hope set before us..." (Hebrews 6:18) "For God is not the author of confusion but of peace..." (1 Corinthians 14:33).

To illustrate this point, let's say we take a Stanley tape measure and measure the length of a table. The tape measure reads four feet in length. Now, do you believe that table is four feet in length? You say, "Of course, that is what it says." Essentially what you are saying is that you have complete faith that the Stanley Company has provided you with a trustworthy standard for measuring.

Now then, when we open our Bibles, we read, "He who believes and is baptized will be saved; but he who does not believe will be condemned" (Mark 16:16). Do you believe this to be true? Do you believe Jesus has answered the question, "What must I do to be saved?" Do you have complete faith that He has given you a trustworthy standard by which you can be saved from your sins? Or, do you question what Christ has said, and look to another for a different answer?

One cannot believe God's word is any different than God's person. If God is trustworthy, so too must be His word. We have trust in the Bible because we have trust in God. A person that does not trust the Bible is a person that does not trust God. A person that does not honor the Bible and keep its sayings is a person that does not honor God.

Our response and respect for God's word essentially and accurately depicts the response and respect we have for God. We must receive God's word with meekness (James 1:21), as we are to receive God with meekness. We must become doers of that word which we meekly receive (James 1:22), because this is a faithful and obedient response to God.

The Savior once asked, "But why do you call me, 'Lord, Lord,' and do not the things which I say?" (Luke 6:46) You see, it is terribly inconsistent to call Him your Lord while willfully disobeying and rejecting His word.

CONCLUSION

The Bible truly is unlike every other book known to man. The Bible is the only book that did not originate with man, but with God. It is the "Book Divine." We love the Bible because we love God. We honor the Bible because we honor God. Let us obey the Bible because we desire to obey God.

Many of the world's problems can be mended by yielding to God's word. The world needs the gospel. May we desire His word more than our necessary food (Job 23:12). May we hunger and thirst after righteousness (Matthew 5:6).

Many of religion's problems can be rectified by surrendering to the word of God. Let us abandon anything and everything which is not found in the word of God. Let us unite solely upon His word. Do away with all manmade theological systems and denominations and let us be Christians and Christians only. Only when we return to the Bible and the Bible alone as our sole rule for faith and practice will we speak the same thing, mind the same thing, and there will be no division among us (1 Corinthians 1:10-13; Philippians 3:16-18).

Many of the home's problems can be resolved by submitting to the word of God. Marriages would endure. Children would be happier. More love would be in the home. How much lovelier the home would be if the responsible parties would only vow, "As for me and my house, we shall serve the Lord"!

Beloved, how many of *your* problems could be cured if only *you* would submit to the will of God? Let us make a personal application. Let us determine in our hearts to conform our will to His word and have our grief turned to joy.

"I beseech you therefore, brethren, by the mercies of God, that you present your bodies a living sacrifice, holy, acceptable to God, *which is* your reasonable service. And do not be conformed to this world, but be transformed by the renewing of your mind, that you may prove what *is* that good and acceptable and perfect will of God" (Romans 12:1-2).

OUR NEED FOR THE UNCHANGING GOSPEL

In Galatians chapter one, verses six through nine, we read of Paul's concern for the churches of the region of Galatia and the direction they were moving. Their digression from the gospel through the influence of false teachers caused the great apostle to write: "I marvel that you are turning away so soon from Him who called you in the grace of Christ, to a different gospel, which is not another; but there are some who trouble you and want to pervert the gospel of Christ. But even if we, or an angel from heaven, preach any other gospel to you than what we have preached to you, let him be accursed. As we have said before, so now I say again, if anyone preaches any other gospel to you than what you have received, let him be accursed."

Having read this passage, let us now state our theme for the lesson: "Our Need for the Unchanging Gospel." Mankind needs the unchanging gospel of Christ. Lost souls and souls longing for a better day need the unchanging gospel of the Lord Jesus Christ.

By way of introduction, I believe it is appropriate to say a few words on what the Scriptures teach about the subject of the gospel. When we consider the word *gospel*, we are not just considering the historical facts and subsequent "good news" of the death, burial, and resurrection of Christ as stated by Paul in 1 Corinthians 15:4. Some have taken Paul's words in this verse to reveal the substance of the gospel entirely. However, Paul did not intend that we should take the gospel to mean only these facts. Rather, he said he declared these facts "first of all" (1 Corinthians 15:3).

These facts served as the foundation for the gospel he preached, not its totality. The gospel is founded upon the historical facts of the death, burial, and resurrection of Christ. But, it includes much, much more.

Some would have us to believe that the gospel is merely the facts of Christ's death, burial, and resurrection and that the *doctrine* of the New Testament is something of secondary importance to the gospel. By defining these terms thusly, essentially they are propagating that we can disagree on *doctrine*, but as long as we agree on the *gospel* (as they define it), we can have unity.

The problem with their theory is that it does not consider other essential passages of scripture. We know this because Peter asked, "...what will be the end of those who *do not obey the gospel of God?*" (1 Peter 4:17). Paul understood that not all men have *"obeyed the gospel"* (Romans 10:16). He also taught that upon Christ's return He would take vengeance upon all *"who do not obey the gospel of our Lord Jesus Christ"* (2 Thessalonians 1:8).

These scriptures serve as proof that the gospel must be obeyed; and yet, man cannot obey historical facts. Therefore, there must be more to the substance of the gospel than merely the historical facts of Christ's death, burial, and resurrection.

The word "gospel" is a term synonymous with other such phrases as the "new covenant" and, therefore, any other synonymous phrase such as: "the word of Christ"; "the word of the Lord"; "the word of God"; "the word of truth"; "the engrafted word"; "law of Christ"; "law of liberty"; "doctrine"; "sound doctrine"; "the faith"; etc. Each one of these terms holds the same meaning. Each phrase or term is referring to the doctrine or the teaching of Christ and His apostles. The gospel is that doctrine to which we must give the more earnest heed as, "how shall we escape if we neglect so great a salvation, which at the first began to be spoken by the Lord, and was confirmed to us by those who heard Him, God also bearing witness both with signs and wonders, with various miracles, and gifts of the Holy Spirit, according to His own will?" (see Hebrews 2:1-4).

Being established upon the death, burial, and resurrection, the gospel message, teaching, or doctrine serves as hope for things eternal to the poor in spirit, the meek, and the lowly. The gospel has been given to heal the brokenhearted and set at liberty those captive to sin.

The word of truth is "the gospel of the kingdom" (Matthew 4:23; 9:35; 24:14). One cannot preach the gospel without preaching the kingdom and dominion of Christ.

The gospel is that divine message intended to bring man in "subjection" to the will of God (2 Corinthians 9:13). The gospel is the fundamental belief system wherein the child of God "stands" if he will "keep in memory" its teachings unless he has "believed in vain" (1 Corinthians 15:2).

The gospel must be obeyed "from the heart" and from the "form of doctrine" (Romans 6:17). Whatever we do for God must be done wholeheartedly and sincerely; but it must also be done obediently and from His word. From the heart and from the Bible – this is the *only* way to obey God.

The "everlasting gospel" instructs us to "Fear God and give glory to Him" (Revelation 14:6-7). God's word is everlasting. "The word of the LORD endures forever. Now this is the word which by the gospel was preached to you" (1 Peter 1:25).

Paul stated that the gospel is "the power of God to salvation" (Romans 1:16). The gospel is God's terms for our salvation. Once the gospel is preached, man has the choice to believe, be baptized, and be saved; or disbelieve and be damned (Mark 16:15-16).

51

According to Paul, there is but one gospel and it reveals the righteousness of God and instructs us to live by faith (Romans 1:17). Moreover, it also reveals the wrath of God against "all ungodliness and unrighteousness of men, who suppress the truth in unrighteousness" (Romans 1:18). Having stated some facts about the nature and purpose of the gospel, let us now turn our attention to our need for the unchanging gospel.

TO OVERCOME WORRY AND SORROW

We need the unchanging gospel because times of worry and sorrow will never completely depart from our lives. We will always be faced with a worry or sorrow of some kind. The fact that our hearts will be broken from time to time does not change. And yet, our hope remains that every time, not just some of the time, but every time we are faced with worry and sorrow we can turn to the gospel, that glorious message of hope, and have our spirits lifted with encouragement from God's own word.

We can rejoice always in the Lord because we have the unchanging gospel with its never-changing ability to lift our spirits and heal our broken hearts with thoughts of eternal peace and everlasting joy. As our faith is established through the gospel, our hearts are warmed by "God's Unchanging Hand." Indeed,

Time is filled with swift transition,
Naught of earth unmoved can stand,
Build your hopes on things eternal,
Hold to God's unchanging hand.

TO OVERCOME TRIBULATION AND PERSECUTION

Secondly, we need the unchanging gospel of Christ because the tribulation and persecution we will face for being a child of God is ever present. Paul instructed Timothy, "Yes, and all who desire to live godly in Christ Jesus will suffer persecution" (2 Timothy 3:12). Peter wrote, "Yet if any man suffer as a Christian, let him not be ashamed; but let him glorify God on this behalf" (1 Peter 4:16).

Even amidst persecution, the gospel is unchanging. It is by our faith in God and His word that we can overcome the persecutions and tribulations that beset us. The martyred Christians whose story is told in the Revelation are heard shouting in heaven: "Now salvation, and strength, and the kingdom of our God, and the power of His Christ have come, for the accuser of our brethren, who accused them before our God day and night, has been cast down. And they overcame him by the blood of the Lamb and by the word of their testimony, and they did not love their lives to the death" (Revelation 12:10-11).

These souls overcame the accuser by the blood of the Lamb, the word of their testimony (the gospel), and by keeping their eyes focused on the life to come rather than living for the here and now. This is a sure strategy for successfully overcoming tribulations in the Christian life! We also can overcome and do all things through the Christ who strengthens (Philippians 4:13). "What then shall we say to these things? If God is for us, who can be against us?" (Romans 8:31)

TO OVERCOME EVIL ALLUREMENTS

Just as we need the unchanging gospel to help us handle unchanging worries and tribulations, we also need the unchanging gospel to overcome the evil allurements Satan will use to tempt us. While the kinds of temptation may differ and change, man will never be fully free from all temptations in this life.

You will always be tempted by something or someone, and you will always need the unchanging gospel to admonish and encourage you. "Submit yourselves therefore to God. Resist the devil, and he will flee from you." While we live with ever-present temptations, we can also live within the ever-present care of a faithful God and Father.

We read in 1 Corinthians 10:13 that "No temptation has overtaken you except such as is common to man; but God is faithful, who will not allow you to be tempted beyond what you are able, but with the temptation will also make the way of escape, that you may be able to bear it."

The gospel reveals the way of escape. Consider how many temptations would cease if we would simply resolve to live in the setting of a proper Christian environment.

Think how many temptations would forever leave our homes if we resolved to make them Christian homes, based solely upon the doctrines of Christ! How many temptations would leave our minds if we resolved to read only good books – especially "The Good Book," watch only good television programs, and avoid any setting or friendship that would entice sin in our hearts?

Think how much happier people would be if they were devoted to the gospel principles of love and encouragement. Think how many marriages would endure rather than ending in divorce if the virtue of forgiveness was practiced.

How many times could sin have been avoided and temptations overcome in our lives, if we would have only done like Joseph when he was confronted by Potiphar's wife, and simply shunned that person or situation that was tempting us? When that wicked woman cast her eyes upon Joseph and said, "Lie with me," it could have been very easy for Joseph to accept her offer. Chances are, Potiphar would have never found out. But Joseph had a conscience, and he knew what was right. Regardless of whether or not Potiphar ever knew what happened, God would know. Joseph answered the temptress saying, "How then can I do this great wickedness, and sin against God?" (Genesis 39:9)

Do you also recall how this wicked woman lied against Joseph and falsely accused him of trying to seduce her? That's the way wicked people will turn on you! That's what she did. Her lying actions and accusations caused Joseph to be cast into one of the Pharaoh's dungeons, "But the Lord was with Joseph, and showed him mercy, and gave him favor in the sight of the keeper of the prison" (Genesis 39:21).

Humble yourselves in the sight of the Lord, and He shall lift you up! Joseph was eventually exalted to the right hand of Egypt. He went from the dungeon of Pharaoh to his right hand. It takes God to do that! He can also lift you up, if you will trust in Him, and let His gospel guide your conscience and determine your actions.

TO OVERCOME THE TACTICS OF SATAN

Also consider how Satan's tactics never change. He is just as lying, deceiving, and conniving as he was in the garden. He will lie to you. He will make you chase a forbidden fruit that will only lead you farther and farther away from God.

He will find your weakness and attempt to fill your heart with envy and doubt. Just as he deceived Eve and Adam, he will attempt to deceive you. He has sent his false teachers out into this world to pervert the gospel of Christ, and we must oppose them with the unchanging truth of the gospel.

The churches of Galatia were facing their problems because of such false teachers. Moreover, many of the problems Christians are facing today are because of false teachers and the distorted picture of the gospel their false doctrines portray.

Satan would have the church to believe and trust doctrines not found in the Bible. He would have every soul on earth belonging to churches and offering worship never authorized by God. All the while, he will continue telling that same old lie of "no consequences for your actions." He told this lie to Eve in the garden when he said, "Thou shalt not surely die."

All Satan had to do was add one word to what God had said to pervert the truth and teach a lie. He was wrong then and he is wrong today. To refuse the brightness of the light of the gospel is to remain in the darkness of Satan's lies.

TO OVERCOME SIN

We also need the unchanging gospel of Christ because we remain weak and prone to sin. We need the unchanging gospel to teach us how we might be forgiven by the grace of an unchanging Savior. Jesus Christ "remains the same yesterday, today, and forever" (Hebrews 13:8). His forgiveness abides still and will abide until He comes again.

While certain things may change, come, and go, the purpose for the gospel remains the same. It remains the word of reconciliation given by God to save our souls. Because of its purpose, the need for the gospel has never changed. Mankind is found in the same condition today as we have been since the garden. "All we like sheep have gone astray; we have turned every one to his own way..." (Isaiah 53:6, KJV). We need a Savior. Jesus Christ is that Savior and the gospel is His power, His authority, to save.

Man cannot be saved without the gospel. "What shall be the end of those who do not obey the gospel of God?" (1 Peter 4:17) The Lord shall come "in flaming fire taking

56

vengeance on those who do not know God, and those who do not obey the gospel of our Lord Jesus Christ. These shall be punished with everlasting destruction from the presence of the Lord, and from the glory of His power..." (2 Thessalonians 1:7-9). Paul is teaching us that to know God is to obey the gospel of the Lord Jesus Christ.

Do you know God? Have you obeyed the gospel of His dear Son? The result of the gospel has never changed. If man will only obey the gospel the hope of heaven shall be his. We hope to see you in that beautiful home of the soul. We invite you to lay hold of eternal life by obeying the unchanging gospel of the Son of God.

CONCLUSION

We need the unchanging gospel because certain evils will never change this side of eternity. Therefore, we see the necessity for unchanging good – the unchanging gospel. Yet, many things in life may change: such as our age, health, jobs, families, and even residences. All of which prompts the need for certainty – for that which will not change. The gospel provides such stability to the life of the believer. "All flesh is as grass, and all the glory of man as the flower of the grass. The grass withers, and its flower falls away, But the word of the LORD endures forever. Now this is the word which by the gospel was preached to you" (1 Peter 1:24-25).

When you need the hand of a stable friend to lift you, turn to Jesus and His word. When you need sound advice for a difficult problem, turn to Christ and His gospel. When everything in life may seem to be crumbling beneath your feet and you feel helpless and have no control, allow God to take control. When you do so, you are taking advantage of the unchanging gospel of Jesus Christ.

THE ANATOMY OF A LOST MAN

The worst thing that can be said of someone's soul is that it is "lost." If a person is lost, it is solely because of the sins that person has committed causing separation from God. God is not to blame for a person being lost. The ugly doctrine of Calvinism would have you to believe that God predestined some to be lost before the world began. According to this false doctrine, these helpless and hopeless souls are going to be lost forever, and there is nothing God, Christ, and they can do to change it. Nowhere does the Bible teach this Calvinistic doctrine. Jesus Christ can save every man (1Timothy 4:10; Hebrews 2:10; 1 John 2:1-2), yet only the one who comes unto Christ in humble obedience will be saved (Hebrews 5:8-9).

Every man could be saved, but not everyone will be saved (Matthew 7:13, 14; 21-23). The saved will be saved because they came to the Lord through penitent and obedient faith. The lost will be lost because they chose not to turn to God. Yet, their decision is not the fault of God. "The Lord is not slack concerning his promise, as some men count slackness; but is longsuffering to us-ward, not willing that any should perish, but that all should come to repentance" (2 Peter 3:9). While Calvinism teaches us that God will not love and refuses to save, the Bible teaches us that "God so loved" in order that He might save!

Adam is not to blame, as some would suppose with the false doctrine of original sin. The Westminster Confession of Faith states:

> "By this sin they (Adam and Eve, *ADE*) fell from their original righteousness and communion with God, and so became dead in sin, and wholly defiled

in all the parts and faculties of soul and body. They being the root of all mankind, the guilt of this sin was imputed; and the same death in sin, and corrupted nature, conveyed to all their posterity descending from them by ordinary generation. From this original corruption, whereby we are utterly indisposed, disabled, and made opposite of all good, and wholly inclined to all evil, do proceed all actual transgressions."[1]

Now read with me from Ezekiel 18:20: "The soul who sins shall die (Not, "the soul who is born in sin" ADE). The son shall not bear the guilt of the father, nor the father bear the guilt of the son. The righteousness of the righteous shall be upon himself, and the wickedness of the wicked shall be upon himself."

From this reading, we learn that the son does not bear the iniquity of the father, nor does the father bear the iniquity of the son. Every man stands for his own actions. Nowhere do we read of a person being judged for the sin of Adam or any other man, for that matter. Paul said, "For we must all appear before the judgment seat of Christ, that each one may receive the things done in the body, according to what he has done, whether good or bad" (2 Corinthians 5:10). Solomon wrote, "For God will bring every work into judgment, including every secret thing, whether it is good or whether it is evil" (Ecclesiastes 12:14).

When I stand before Christ at the Final Judgment, I will be giving an account for the things I have done. God will render to "each one according to his deeds" (Romans 2:6). The Lord has said, "And behold, I am coming quickly, and

---

[1] The Westminster Confession of Faith, Chapter VI, "Of the Fall of Man, Of Sin and of the Punishment Thereof," Parts II, III, and IV.

My reward is with Me, to give to every one according to his work" (Revelation 22:12). Nowhere does the Bible teach that a man will be judged for the sins of another. The Bible teaches that every man will be judged for his own doings – whether good or bad.

I find it to be terribly inconsistent for a Calvinistic preacher to chastise his flock for not doing enough good works, or for being too worldly-minded, when according to his doctrine these people are only doing what they have been programmed to do. Calvinists deny that we have free-will. We are nothing more than mindless robots, doing as we have been programmed to do by God, according to Calvinism.

However, the Bible teaches us to, "Let no one say when he is tempted, 'I am tempted by God'; for God cannot be tempted by evil, nor does He Himself tempt anyone. But each one is tempted when he is drawn away by his own de-sires and enticed. Then, when desire has conceived, it gives birth to sin; and sin, when it is full-grown, brings forth death" (James 1:13-15).

Only *you* are responsible for the condition of your soul. Read with me from Ezekiel 18:21-24, "But if a wicked man turns from all his sins which he has committed, keeps all My statutes, and does what is lawful and right, he shall surely live; he shall not die. None of the transgressions which he has committed shall be remembered against him; because of the righteousness which he has done, he shall live. 'Do I have any pleasure at all that the wicked should die?' says the Lord God, 'and not that he should turn from his ways and live?' But when a righteous man turns away from his right-eousness and commits iniquity, and does according to all the abominations that the wicked man does, shall he live? All the righteousness which he has done shall not be remem-bered; because of the unfaithfulness of which he is guilty

61

and the sin which he has committed, because of them he shall die."

It is not enough to turn from sin. We must turn from sin and turn to God. A man can turn from sin for any number of reasons. Perhaps he wants to be a better husband, father, or son. Maybe he is tired of the consequences of sin. But, unless he turns to God, he cannot be forgiven.

Finding forgiveness is not a matter of doing more good than bad, or less bad than good. There will be no set of scales on the Judgment Day used to weigh the deeds of a person to see if they measure up. If man could be saved that way, why did Christ have to die?

The passage we have just read states that God will not remember one single good deed the backslider has performed. Neither will He remember one single sin the converted man has committed. You will either be completely saved or completely lost. Man is either 100% saved or 100% lost. There is no in between.

Finding forgiveness is not a matter of doing more good than bad or less bad than good. For the man who lives righteously, there will be nothing bad remembered of him. God will forever blot those things from His book of remembrance. For the man who has lived wickedly, there will be nothing good remembered about him. Any good deeds he may have done will also be blotted from that divine book.

We have here, in this lesson, the anatomy of a lost man. It is important for a lost man to know why he is lost and what he must do to be forgiven. The lost soul is lost for a reason. Those reasons have led to his sad condition. If the lost will learn the reasons for his lost state, and correct those things that are amiss in his life, as God told Ezekiel, he can "turn from all his sins and live."

THE LOST MIND

The first organ I would like to introduce in the anatomy of a lost man is the mind. The lost mind has become ruined, warped, and twisted by the carnal passions of a world that has embraced evil and hated good. Paul describes the lost man's mind in this way: "And even as they did not like to retain God in their knowledge, God gave them over to a debased mind, to do those things which are not fitting; being filled with all unrighteousness, sexual immorality, wickedness, covetousness, maliciousness; full of envy, murder, strife, deceit, evil-mindedness; they are whisperers, backbiters, haters of God, violent, proud, boasters, inventors of evil things, disobedient to parents, undiscerning, untrustworthy, unloving, unforgiving, unmerciful; who, knowing the righteous judgment of God, that those who practice such things are worthy of death, not only do the same but also approve of those who practice them" (Romans 1:28-32).

The lost mind has been enslaved by a satanic rule and will not submit to the will of God. The lost man is carnally minded and "the carnal mind is enmity against God; for it is not subject to the law of God, nor indeed can be" (Romans 8:7). It is filled with futile vanity (Ephesians 4:17). It has become defiled by the garbage it has absorbed. The old saying "garbage in – garbage out" applies here. "To the pure all things are pure, but to those who are defiled and unbelieving nothing is pure; but even their mind and conscience are defiled" (Titus 1:15).

THE LOST EYES

The eyes of the lost soul have helped to warp the mind. Such eyes have been intentionally closed to the truth. They see but do not perceive. "For the heart of this people has grown dull. their ears are hard of hearing, and their eyes *they have closed*, lest they should see with their eyes and hear with their ears, lest they should understand with their heart and turn, so that I should heal them" (Acts 28:27).

Rather than focusing on the truth and the things that are pure and lovely, the lost man focuses his eyes upon lustful things. "The lust of the eyes" (1 John 2:16) is all that captures his attention. Such eyes have become "full of adultery" (2 Peter 2:14).

Lost souls refuse to make "a covenant with their eyes" (Job 31:1). To be cured, the lost must anoint their eyes with salve (Revelation 3:18) – yea even the balm of Gilead!

THE LOST EARS

The ears of the lost man are just as deplorable as his eyes. His ears have conveniently become "hard of hearing" as he refuses to listen to the gospel (Acts 28:17). He has what you might call "selective hearing."

He hears what he wants to hear. As his ears desire to be tickled they are turned away from the truth, even unto the fables of men (2 Timothy 4:3-4). He can hear the fables, the doctrines and commandments of men, but when it comes to hearing the truth *then* he stubbornly becomes dull of hearing.

Isaiah encountered lost ears when dealing with the rebellion in Israel. The Lord said to His prophet, "Now go, write it before them on a tablet, And note it on a scroll, That it may be for time to come, Forever and ever: That this is a rebellious people, Lying children, Children who will not hear the law of the Lord; Who say to the seers, 'Do not see,' And to the prophets, 'Do not prophesy to us right things; Speak to us smooth things, prophesy deceits. Get out of the way. Turn aside from the path, Cause the Holy One of Israel to cease from before us'" (Isaiah 30:9-10).

We are living in the midst of rebellious people today as well. They stop their ears to truth and will only listen to "smooth things." They have no interest in hearing "right things" or in yielding to the law of the Lord.

THE LOST TONGUE

Moreover, the lost soul's tongue has not been bridled. His religion, if he has any, is useless. For, "If anyone among you thinks he is religious, and does not bridle his tongue but deceives his own heart, this one's religion is useless" (James 1:26).

His tongue is not controlled, you see. Therefore, it defiles his whole body, and is set on a course for hell (James 3:6). James also says this type of forked tongue is used both to bless and to curse. Read with me, "Out of the same mouth proceed blessing and cursing. My brethren, these things ought not to be so" (James 3:10).

THE LOST HANDS

The lost man's hands deny God with their works. "They profess to know God, but in works they deny Him, being abominable, disobedient, and disqualified for every good work" (Titus 1:16).

The lost must cleanse his hands and purify his heart (James 4:8). By the works of his hands, he has caused himself to be lost and has destroyed his relationship with the Father.

THE LOST KNEES

Let's look now at the knees which are never bent in prayer. No, the lost man will not humbly bow in prayer, but he seemingly has no problem bowing to anything and everything his wicked heart desires! He bows his knees to the idolatrous altar of covetousness (Colossians 3:5), rather than the throne of Almighty God.

Paul instructed Timothy to "Command those who are rich in this present age not to be haughty, nor to trust in uncertain riches but in the living God, who gives us richly all things to enjoy. Let them do good, that they be rich in good works, ready to give, willing to share, storing up for themselves a good foundation for the time to come, that they may lay hold on eternal life" (1 Timothy 6:17-19).

THE LOST FEET

The lost man has feet which are swift in running to carry out the wicked imaginations of his foolish heart (Proverbs 6:18). Because he is walking in darkness, he does not know his way and cannot see where he is going (John 12:35). He errs in vision and stumbles in judgment (Isaiah 28:7). He would rather stumble through the darkness of this world's defilements and degeneration than walk in the light of the God who loves him.

THE LOST HEART

Perhaps more than any other component of the lost man's anatomy, it is important for us to discuss the lost man's heart. It is because the heart has not been given wholly to God that the mind, eyes, ears, tongue, hands, knees, and feet act as wickedly as they do.

The debased treasures proceeding from a profane heart have defiled the lost man. Jesus has taught us, "For from within, out of the heart of men, proceed evil thoughts, adulteries, fornications, murders, thefts, covetousness, wickedness, deceit, licentiousness, an evil eye, blasphemy, pride, foolishness. All these evil things come from within and defile a man" (Mark 7:18-23).

Though the lost man may choose to honor God with his lips, his hypocritical heart is far from Him (Matthew 15:8). The lost heart is blinded by ignorance (Ephesians 4:18). It has become foolishly darkened (Romans 1:21). Such a heart is filled with bitter envy and strife, rather than the wisdom from above (James 3:14-16). For some lost men, it foolishly tells them, "There is no God" (Psalm 53:1).

The lost heart has become evil, departing from the living God, even hardening itself through the deceitfulness of sin. For this very reason, brethren beloved, we are admonished, "Beware, brethren, lest there be in any of you an evil heart of unbelief in departing from the living God; but exhort one another daily, while it is called 'Today,' lest any of you be hardened through the deceitfulness of sin" (Hebrews 3:12-13).

CONCLUSION

Thus you have the anatomy of a lost man. Wickedness reigns from the crown of his head to the soles of his feet. If he were to shed his mortal robe as he sits right now, his eternity would doubtlessly cast a dark, grim, and never-ending shadow. How awful it would be to be lost for all eternity!

As we stated before, the utter deplorableness of the lost man's state is not questionable. Neither do we question how he came into this condition. We know that God loves him and longs to see him repent. We also know that all those who love God and love the souls of men would love to see him change and correct the causes of his sad condition. But, what does remain to be seen is whether or not the lost soul will care enough about his soul to make those necessary changes.

Will the wicked turn from his wickedness? Is there no shame for the actions he has done? Will he not show sorrow for the sins that have broken His Savior's heart? Will the reprobate mind decide to learn the truth and learn to focus on the beauty of the cross, rather than the ugliness of sin? Will closed eyes and ears be opened to the power of the gospel?

Will the tongue that now speaks lies and envious hatred begin to speak the good news of the gospel of Christ? Will the hands whose deeds shame the man become busy working the works of righteousness? Will the lost man come to believe that we are meant to be "His workmanship, created in Christ Jesus for good works, which God prepared beforehand that we should walk in them"?

Will the knees that stubbornly refuse to bend in prayerful submission learn to bow? Will the feet that are now swift to mischief become swift to worship, swift to Bible study, swift to righteousness, and swift to save the lost? Will these feet be swift to obey the gospel?

Indeed, the heart that was once far from God can be reconciled by the blood of Christ. That hardened pulsating stone can be pricked to ask tearfully, "What must I do to be saved?" Just as the lost are lost because of the poor decisions they have made, so too are the saved redeemed by the wise decisions they have made. Saved people are saved because they decided to do something about their sins. They decided to yield in humble obedience to the gospel of God's dear Son. The saved are saved because they have decided to turn to God through the blood of His dear Son.

Dear soul, fix your eyes upon the sunlit lanes of eternity. Care as much for your soul as does your Savior. Learn to consider things in terms of good and evil. Surely you do not want to be considered an evil man! All of your sins can be forgotten and erased (Hebrews 10:17). We invite you to turn from the path of destruction and eternal despair to begin a blessed walk in the light of God's dear Son.

Hear the gospel and believe it. Jesus died for you. He has been raised to the right hand of His Father in heaven. He rules over His spiritual kingdom – the church – waiving His scepter of righteousness even now. Repent of your sins. You must turn from sin and turn to your God. It is not enough to turn from sin. You must turn *to* God. Confess your conviction that Jesus is the Son of God and be baptized for the remission of sin calling upon the name of the Lord (Acts 2:38; Acts 22:16).

BAPTISM STANDS BETWEEN

"There is one Lord, one faith, and one baptism" (Ephesians 4:5). Our lesson will attempt to teach the significance of the "one baptism" mentioned by Paul and by other writers of the New Testament. When we speak of this baptism, we are speaking of a burial in water. The New Testament declares such to be the case in Romans 6:3-4 and Colossians 2:12. That this burial occurs in water is declared in 1 Peter 3:20-21 as well as accounts of conversion in the book of Acts (cf. Acts 8:36-39).

In English we have three words signifying three distinct actions. These words are: immerse, sprinkle, and pour. So also in the New Testament, we have three Greek words denoting three separate actions. These words are: *baptisma* is transliterated *baptism* in English. The root word for *baptisma* is *bapto*, which means "to dip, to dip in, to plunge, to bury, to cover up, to immerse." As we have noted, Paul defined baptism as a burial (Romans 6:3-4; Colossians 2:12-13).

While Webster's Dictionary cites baptism to be immersion, sprinkling, or pouring, the New Testament tells a different story. Had the inspired writers desired to command the sprinkling or pouring of water, rather than an immersion in water, two perfectly acceptable words could have been chosen – *rhantizo* (to sprinkle), and *cheo* (to pour).

One last thought on this point: a person can be immersed in or into water as the Bible teaches, but person cannot be sprinkled or poured in or into water. Such would obviously render the actions of sprinkling and pouring impossible. By way of introduction, I would also like for you to observe that the title for the lesson is "Baptism Stands Between." You will notice that we are not saying "the sinner's prayer

stands between" or, "the mourner's bench stands between."
If we could find either of these things in the New Testament,
then we would have grounds for such a study. But, seeing
that neither the prayer nor the bench stands between the sinner and salvation according to the gospel, we shall study that
which *does* stand between in studying baptism.

BAPTISM STANDS BETWEEN THE BELIEVER AND BEING SAVED

The words of Jesus on the subject of baptism have been
forever recorded in Mark's record: "Go into all the world
and preach the gospel to every creature. He who believes
and is baptized will be saved; but he who does not believe
will be condemned" (Mark 16:15-16). You will observe that
these are the words Christ spoke to His disciples, those who
would be charged with making disciples of all nations, just
before He ascended into heaven to the right hand of the
throne of God.

According to Jesus Christ, "He that believes and is baptized will be saved..." It was the will of Christ that the
command of baptism should stand between the conviction of
believing the proclaimed gospel and the promise of being
saved.

It could be that you have never been taught these words
of Christ. It could be that you have been taught quite the
opposite. Possibly you have heard some strong and convincing sermons which have led you to believe that baptism
is not essential to being saved. If that is the case, I would
like for you to grant me one request and, in your mind's eye,
I would like for you to picture a set of balances. Do you
have the balances clearly pictured? On the one side I would
like for you to place every sermon, testimony, or statement
you have ever heard that is contrary to or would negate or

72

reject the importance of baptism to your salvation. Place every "sinner's prayer" you've heard on this side of the scales. Place every preacher you have ever heard say man is saved by faith alone, and that baptism is a work of men, on this side of the scales. Go ahead and picture how heavy you believe the evidence to be against the case for baptism in God's plan of salvation.

On the other side of your scale, I would like for you to place this one, single, solitary statement of the Lord Jesus Christ, "He that believes and is baptized shall be saved." No other man, no other sermon, no other statement is needed.

Who do you believe? In the court of your conscience, does the testimony of Christ have the greater influence? Or, are you going to allow the words, testimonies, and doctrines of men to determine your judgment? Will you believe God or men? Who are you willing to trust with your soul? Who are going to follow?

I have heard people argue against this passage by saying that Jesus did not say, "He who is not baptized shall be damned." Jesus did not have to say this. He said, "He that does not believe will be damned." If a person does not believe, they certainly are not going to be a candidate for baptism.

It would be the same as if I said, "He that eats and digests shall live. He that does not eat shall die." Who shall live? What is required in order to live? That man must eat *and* digest – he must do both – if he wants to live. Who shall die? The one who does not eat shall die. Why did I not say "He who does not eat and does not digest shall die"? A person isn't going to digest food if he hasn't eaten. And, a person isn't going to be baptized if he hasn't believed.

Now, let us get back to the original question, who is going to be saved? The Lord Jesus Christ said, "He that believes and is baptized shall be saved." This command applies to every person living in the Christian age. It is a message to be preached to every creature (Mark 16:15), and until the end of the world (Matthew 28:18-20).

BAPTISM STANDS BETWEEN THE PENITENT PERSON AND THE FORGIVENESS OF SINS

In the second chapter of Acts, we find the disciples doing just as Christ commanded – preaching the gospel. At the summit of Peter's first gospel sermon, as he stood and boldly proclaimed the death, burial, and resurrection of Christ for the first time, the Jews who heard that sermon were cut in their hearts and cried, "Men and brethren, what shall we do?" (Acts 2:37)

What do you suppose they wanted to know? Suppose this had been you, and you were told you were guilty of crucifying the Son of God. What do you suppose you would have wanted to know?

Peter's answer is found beginning in verse thirty-eight, "Repent, and let every one of you be baptized in the name of Jesus Christ for the remission of sins; and you shall receive the gift of the Holy Spirit... Then those who gladly received his word were baptized; and that day about three thousand souls were added to them" (Acts 2:38, 41). You will observe that baptism stood between these believers and their forgiveness. Upon their repentance, they were commanded to be baptized for the forgiveness of their sins.

They cried out, "What shall we do?" Peter answered, "Repent and let every one of you be baptized in the name of Jesus Christ for the remission of sins..." Peter was telling them how to save themselves from a perverse generation (Acts 2:40); and this very command applies to those living in this perverse generation today.

74

From Acts 2 to Revelation 22, nothing changed in God's plan of salvation. The commandment to repent and be baptized for the remission of sin abides still – unto our children and our children's children, "as many as the Lord our God shall call."

BAPTISM STANDS BETWEEN THE PENITENT BELIEVER WHO HAS CONFESSED CHRIST AND THE FORGIVENESS OF SINS

Let us consider the conversion of Saul of Tarsus. He would come to be known as the apostle Paul (Acts 13:9). He would later confess that he was once the chief of sinners (1 Timothy 1:15), and that by his conversion a pattern was given to all that would believe unto life everlasting (1 Timothy 1:16).

We can read of his conversion in Acts chapters nine, twenty-two, and twenty-six. From reading these accounts we learn how Saul of Tarsus was on his way to Damascus in order to bring Christians to trial and punishment for their faith. The Lord appeared to him on the road to Damascus and inquired of these persecutions.

Saul was blinded by a great light radiating from the heavenly vision of Christ, and trembling and astonished he cried out, "Lord, what do You want me to do?" (Acts 9:6) Christ told him to go to Damascus and there it would be told him what he "*must* do."

I'd like to call to your attention the fact that Saul was in Damascus for *three days* praying and fasting until Ananias was sent by the Lord to tell him what he must do (Acts 9:9, 11). After three days of praying and fasting, Ananias laid his hands on Saul so that he might recover his sight. He then recovered the sight he lost when he was blinded by the heavenly light. Ananias then told Saul, "And now why are you waiting? Arise and be baptized, and wash away your sins, calling on the name of the Lord (Acts 22:16).

Loved ones, do consider if *three days* of prayer and fasting did not wash away Saul's sins, how can a three minute "sinner's prayer" wash away your sins? It has been claimed that Saul was saved on the Damascus road. If so, whose sins did he wash away three days later?

I once had a denominational preacher tell me that Saul washed away the sins of his daily walk when he was baptized. He thought he was being clever and attempting to hang on to his belief that Saul was saved at the point of faith. However, in actuality he merely admitted that God uses baptism as part of His requirements to wash away sins. According to the conversion of Saul, which is "a pattern to those who are going to believe on Him for everlasting life," baptism stands between the penitent believer and washing away sins.

BAPTISM STANDS BETWEEN
THE OLD LIFE AND THE NEW LIFE

In Romans chapter six we learn how a person dies with Christ, is buried with Christ, and is raised with Christ to live a new life. Read with me, "Or do you not know that as many of us as were baptized into Christ Jesus were baptized into His death? Therefore we were buried with Him through baptism into death, that just as Christ was raised from the dead by the glory of the Father, even so we also should walk in newness of life" (Romans 6:3-4).

By *baptism*, we become united with Christ and are brought into harmony and spiritual union with His death, burial, and resurrection. Continue reading from this chapter, verses five through seven: "For if we have been united together in the likeness of His death, certainly we also shall be

76

in the likeness of His resurrection, knowing this, that our old man was crucified with Him, that the body of sin might be done away with, that we should no longer be slaves of sin. For he who has died has been freed from sin."

According to Paul, baptism stands between the sinner and being freed from his sins. By being baptized into His death, you have the promise of being in the likeness of His resurrection, destroying the old man of sin, and thus being freed from the bondage of sin. God has selected the action of baptism to signify the point in which we are united with the death, burial, and resurrection of Christ. One cannot obey the gospel of the death, burial, and resurrection of Christ without being baptized. One cannot be resurrected unto a new man without a death and burial of the old man.

BAPTISM STANDS BETWEEN BEING A CHILD OF THE DEVIL AND A CHILD OF GOD

Let us continue in the writings of Paul by reading Galatians 3:26-27. "For you are all sons of God through faith in Christ Jesus. For as many of you as were baptized into Christ have put on Christ."

Many of our religious friends will read verse twenty-six without reading verse twenty-seven. We are children of God by faith in Christ Jesus. Our question is *when* do we become children of God by faith in Christ Jesus? You will observe from this passage that baptism stands between the sinner and becoming a son of God through faith in Christ Jesus. Moreover, baptism stands between a person being in or out of Christ. It stands between your being clothed with Christ or remaining defiled in the sin-stained garments of this world.

BAPTISM STANDS BETWEEN BEING
ALIVE IN CHRIST OR DEAD IN SIN

Let us now read Colossians 2:11-13. Paul writes, "In Him you were also circumcised with the circumcision made without hands, by putting off the body of the sins of the flesh, by the circumcision of Christ, buried with Him in baptism, in which you also were raised with Him through faith in the working of God, who raised Him from the dead. And you, being dead in your trespasses and the uncircumcision of your flesh, He has made alive together with Him, having forgiven you all trespasses..."

I believe this passage is one of the most powerful passages we could include in a sermon on baptism. From this passage you will observe that baptism stands between man and (1) putting off the body of the sins of the flesh; (2) being buried with Christ; (3) being raised with Christ through faith in the operation of God; (4) being made alive together with Him; and (5) being forgiven of all trespasses. You will note that Paul has said essentially the same thing and made the same key points pertaining to baptism in this passage as in Romans 6:3-7.

Also, you will observe that baptism is not a work of men, but "the working of God." Many have rejected the spiritual significance of baptism because they have been led to believe baptism is a work of men, and man is not saved by works (Ephesians 2:8-10). However, even belief is a work. The disciples once asked Jesus what they might do to work the works of God. Jesus answered them saying, "This is the work of God, that you believe in Him whom He sent" (John 6:28-29). Thus, believing in Jesus is a work! But, neither belief nor baptism is a work of the old law, which happens to be the works under discussion in Ephesians 2:8-10.

78

BAPTISM STANDS BETWEEN
BEING SAVED AND BEING UNSAVED

Lastly, I would like to call your attention to a passage written by Peter, 1 Peter 3:20-22. Beginning midway through verse twenty we read, "...in the days of Noah, while the ark was being prepared, in which a few, that is, eight souls, were saved through water. There is also an antitype which now saves us—baptism (not the removal of the filth of the flesh, but the answer of a good conscience toward God), through the resurrection of Jesus Christ, who has gone into heaven and is at the right hand of God, angels and authorities and powers having been made subject to Him." The King James Version reads, "...baptism doth also now save us."

It is not the removal of any dirt or filth in the process of being baptized that saves man. I am not telling you the water saves you. I do not believe there is any cleansing power inherently in the water of baptism. I know that it is the blood of Christ that cleanses you of your sins.

However, baptism stands between you and being cleansed by that blood. Baptism, according to Peter, occurs when a person appeals to God out of a good conscience and sincere heart.

Paul teaches us that when we are baptized we are "obeying from the heart the form of doctrine which has been delivered to us" (Romans 6:17); and, "being *then* made free from sins, you became the servants of righteousness" (Romans 6:18).

CONCLUSION

It is not sufficient that I merely attempt to convince of the biblical truth of baptism. As a gospel preacher, I must attempt to convert you to Christ. By now you understand what baptism stands between. God's commandment is not given to divide you from Him, or His church, but to bridge the gap. Allow the hand of Christ to help you to cross that bridge. Come out of darkness and into His marvelous light.

When you are scripturally baptized, you are pledging your life to Christ. You are joining yourself to Him in His new covenant. He will forgive you of every sin and add you to His church (Acts 2:42, 47). Beloved, such mercy and grace is extended to you now. Today truly is the day of salvation.

CAN A CHILD OF GOD FALL FROM GRACE?

Our theme for this study is perhaps the most needed lesson for a child of God to learn, especially the child of God who has returned to living in sin. We shall be studying what New Testament teaches about falling away or apostasy. This theme could be stated many ways. It would carry the same meaning if we were to ask, "Can a child of God so sin as to fall from grace?" You could also see the point if we were to ask, "Can a child of God – a saved person – so sin as to be eternally lost?"

What we are discussing is the possibility of apostasy. Paul speaks on a great apostasy or "falling away" in 2 Thessalonians 2:3. Apostasy is "defection from truth." It means "to forsake;" and "to depart from, divorce, or separate." We are asking, "Can a child of God, divorce himself or depart from Christ by returning to the world and the sin thereof?"

Sadly, I fear, there are many more advocating false doctrines on this subject in the religious world than there are to be found teaching the truth. Most likely, we are all at least somewhat familiar with the doctrine of "once saved always saved," as it is commonly called. Some of us may believe it to be true.

The idea is actually very old, though it is not as old as the New Testament. It originated with Augustine (354-430 AD) and reappeared in the 16th Century through the teachings of the French theologian John Calvin. He called it "Perseverance of the Saints."

ANSWERING CALVINISM

Calvinists believe that since man did nothing to secure his salvation, but was chosen to be one of the "elect" by God's sovereign choice, he can do nothing to lose his salvation. While some Calvinists disagree, the hardline followers believe that since man is saved unconditionally, he must also remain saved unconditionally. They do not believe your fate is in your actions, but in God's sovereign grace or election. Accordingly, salvation is solely a matter of whether or not God has predestined you to be lost or saved and that number cannot be changed by even one soul. You have no free-will or choice in the matter of your salvation according to Calvinism.

When we turn to the Bible, however, we can easily learn that a person becomes a child of God by obeying certain conditions or commandments given by God. Even a casual reading of the New Testament will point out such commandments as hearing, believing, repenting, confessing faith in Christ, and being baptized. As you read your Bibles, why not underscore the little two-letter word "if." "If" demonstrates that there are conditions and promises predicated upon our choices. The New Testament is full of passages instructing saints and sinners alike, "If you...then I will..." The idea is simply "if...or else."

Take, for instance, 1 Corinthians 15:1-2: "Moreover, brethren, I declare to you the gospel which I preached to you, which also you received and in which you stand, by which also you are saved, *if* you hold fast that word which I preached to you—*unless* you believed in vain."

Also consider, "...but Christ as a Son over His own house, whose house we are *if* we hold fast the confidence and the rejoicing of the hope firm to the end" (Hebrews 3:6).

Calvinism also maintains that while the child of God may sin outwardly, his inward being has been forever sanctified and regenerated by the blood of Christ and the indwelling of the Holy Spirit. Accordingly, regardless of what the flesh (or outward man) may do, the inner man will remain pure.

82

However, you will observe from the Scriptures that God does indeed hold the child of God accountable for the "sins of the flesh." Note: "Now the works of the flesh are evident, which are: adultery, fornication, uncleanness, lewdness, idolatry, sorcery, hatred, contentions, jealousies, outbursts of wrath, selfish ambitions, dissensions, heresies, envy, murders, drunkenness, revelries, and the like; of which I tell you beforehand, just as I also told you in time past, that those who practice such things *will not inherit the kingdom of God*" (Galatians 5:19-21).

The doctrine of "perseverance of the saints" does not recognize that the works of the flesh will cause the child of God to forfeit his inheritance in the kingdom of God. Sin is a serious matter. Sin will cost the child of God his salvation. "Let no one say when he is tempted, 'I am tempted by God'; for God cannot be tempted by evil, nor does He Himself tempt anyone. But each one is tempted when he is drawn away by his own desires and enticed. Then, when desire has conceived, it gives birth to sin; and sin, when it is full-grown, *brings forth death*. Do not be deceived, my beloved brethren" (James 1:13-16).

James not only warns us about the possibility of apostasy, he also gives instructions for helping those who have so erred. "Brethren, if anyone among you wanders (errs, KJV) from the truth, and someone turns him back, let him know that he who turns (converts, KJV) a sinner from the error of his way will save a soul from death and cover a multitude of sins" (James 5:19-20).

Every man will ultimately stand before Christ to be judged for the deeds done *in the body*. "For we must all appear before the judgment seat of Christ, that each one may receive the things done in the body, according to what he has done, whether good or bad. Knowing, therefore, the terror of the Lord, we persuade men; but we are well known to God, and I also trust are well known in your consciences" (2 Corinthians 5:10-11).

Also contrary to Calvinism, the Bible teaches that the inward man *can* sin. Paul wrote, "Therefore, having these promises, beloved, let us cleanse ourselves from all filthiness *of the flesh and spirit*, perfecting holiness in the fear of God." (2 Corinthians 7:1).

Paul would previously write to the same congregation, saying, "For you were bought at a price; therefore glorify God *in your body and in your spirit*, which are God's" (1 Corinthians 6:20). Man is responsible to God for his body *and* his spirit.

Calvin and his followers have a mistaken approach to the Scriptures. They have not considered all the passages fairly and, therefore, have decided to pit one set of passages against another. Anytime a person takes this approach to the text, he is destined to fail in arriving at a sound conclusion. The "perseverance" doctrine requires that we take *only* the passages which teach about the possibility of our security as Christians, while avoiding or falsely interpreting the passages which teach that this security is conditional.

SPECIFIC SINS WHICH BRING CONDEMNATION

Many specific sins can stand between a child of God and the continued blessing of forgiveness. Let me ask you, have you ever considered the Savior's teaching on the subject of forgiving a person who comes to you penitently seeking your forgiveness? Do you realize that if we refuse to forgive a penitent person (Luke 17:2) – especially a brother (see Matthew 18:23-35) – who comes asking our forgiveness, *"neither will your Father in heaven forgive your trespasses"*

84

(Mark 11:26). The refusal to forgive the penitent is a specific sin standing between your sins and God's forgiveness.

Also, have you paused to consider the way you approach the Lord's Supper? Paul wrote, "For as often as you eat this bread and drink this cup, you proclaim the Lord's death till He comes. Therefore whoever eats this bread or drinks this cup of the Lord in an unworthy manner will be guilty of the body and blood of the Lord. But let a man examine himself, and so let him eat of the bread and drink of the cup. For he who eats and drinks in an unworthy manner eats and drinks judgment (damnation, KJV) to himself, not discerning the Lord's body" (1 Corinthians 11:26-29).

The question is not, "Am I worthy enough to partake?" As a child of God in covenant with Him you are commanded to worship in this way. The question is rather, "Am I worshipping in a worthy manner?" Regardless of what you may think, or what you may have heard another say or teach, it *does* matter how you worship God. Your soul is at stake. Make a mockery out of the Lord's Supper and lose your soul. Moreover, it cannot be argued that these people were not saved, for only the saved are commanded to keep the memorial in this way.

Likewise, have you paused to consider the importance of your Lord's Day attendance? The writer of Hebrews admonished thusly: "...not forsaking the assembling of ourselves together, as is the manner of some, but exhorting one another, and so much the more as you see the Day approaching. For if we sin willfully after we have received the knowledge of the truth, there no longer remains a sacrifice for sins, but a certain fearful expectation of judgment, and fiery indignation which will devour the adversaries. Anyone who has rejected Moses' law dies without mercy on the testimony of two or three witnesses. Of how much worse punishment, do you suppose, will he be thought worthy who has trampled the Son of God underfoot, counted the blood of the covenant by which he was sanctified a common thing, and insulted the Spirit of grace? For we know Him who said, 'Vengeance is Mine, I will repay,' says the Lord. And again, 'The LORD will judge His people.' It is a fearful thing to fall into the hands of the living God." (Hebrews 10:25-31).

The Lord will judge His people on the basis of their worship on the Lord's Day. For those who forsake the assembling of themselves together, it is a fearful thing to fall into the hands of the living God. To forsake the assembly is not to miss a service because of illness, work, or vacation. To forsake the assembly is to quit assembling with the saints. When a person has decided to stop worshipping God in the assembly of the church, and has determined to do otherwise, that person has determined to forsake the assembly. It is a willful sin and will go unforgiven unless that person repents.

Any sin (not repented of) can become a sin unto death. John instructs us on this matter. "If anyone sees *his brother* sinning a sin which does not lead to death, he will ask, and He will give him life for those who commit sin not leading to death. There is sin leading to death. I do not say that he should pray about that" (1 John 5:16).

As Christians, we are prohibited from asking God to forgive a brother or sister who is unwilling to repent of their coveted sin. Their coveted sin has become a sin unto death. Lust has conceived sin and sin has brought death – a spiritual separation from God. A brother in this condition must be converted from his sins in order to save his soul from death. Just as the prodigal son had to return for his father to say, "My son who was dead lives again," the erring child of God must return to the fold for him to live again.

SPECIFIC LIFESTYLES WHICH BRING CONDEMNATION

Certain lifestyles will condemn a child of God. Our manner of life should be characterized by holiness and godliness (2 Peter 3:11). However, for many brethren their manner of living can be characterized by such words as were used by Paul when he wrote, "But now I have written to you not to keep company with anyone named a brother, who is sexually immoral, or covetous, or an idolater, or a reviler, or a drunkard, or an extortioner—not even to eat with such a person" (1 Corinthians 5:11).

Adultery is a *condemned* lifestyle (Galatians 5:19). Souls are being manipulated, indoctrinated, and saturated by our culture into believing it is an acceptable lifestyle. Yet, the Bible says it is and work of the flesh and will prevent you from going to heaven.

Covetousness can determine a person's manner of living. In the parable of a covetous farmer or the "rich fool," "God said to him, 'Fool! This night your soul will be required of you; then whose will those things be which you have provided?'" (Luke 12:20). The moral of this parable is stated in the next verse, "So is he that lays up treasure for himself, and is not rich toward God."

On several occasions, Paul forbade and condemned the lifestyle of the drunkard. Man has tried to sooth this sin wishing to make "social drinking" acceptable. Abuse of alcohol and even its recreational use is a great evil. Just look at what it has done to our homes. Just look at how it has ruined so many lives. It is a great evil. Let us avoid the very appearance of evil!

Drunkenness is a work of the flesh and those who commit such things *"shall not inherit the kingdom of God."* "Wine is a mocker, strong drink is a brawler, and whoever is led astray by it (deceived thereby, KJV) is not wise" (Proverbs 20:1). Drinking parties are also sinful (1 Peter 4:3). Even if you are not staggering drunk in such places, you are sinning by being there. God has granted one use for wine and it is *medicinal* not social (1 Timothy 5:23).

The life of the backsliding Christian is forbidden. Consider the backslider. The Lord Himself said, "No one, having put his hand to the plow, and looking back, is fit for the kingdom of God" (Luke 9:62).

Peter speaks to Christians who were being tempted to backslide by false teachers, saying: "For if, after they have escaped the pollutions of the world through the knowledge of the Lord and Savior Jesus Christ, they are again entangled in them and overcome, the latter end is worse for them than the beginning. For it would have been better for them not to have known the way of righteousness, than having known it, to turn from the holy commandment delivered to them. But it has happened to them according to the true proverb: 'A dog returns to his own vomit,' and, 'a sow, having washed, to her wallowing in the mire.'" (2 Peter 2:20-22).

SPECIFIC WORDS WHICH MUST BE STUDIED

If you still need convincing, just take the word "fall" and see how it is used in the New Testament. Paul warned the Corinthians, "Therefore let him who thinks he stands take heed lest he fall" (1 Corinthians 10:12).

Paul wrote to the Galatians who were being tempted to mingle Judaism with Christianity and said, "You have become estranged from Christ, you who attempt to be justified by law; you have fallen from grace" (Galatians 5:4).

Peter warned, "You therefore, beloved, since you know this beforehand, beware lest you also fall from your own steadfastness, being led away with the error of the wicked" (2 Peter 3:17).

The Lord spoke of those who "fall away" in times of temptation (Luke 8:13); and would admonish the brethren in Ephesus to remember from whence they had "fallen" (Revelation 2:1-5).

Now, take the word "depart" and you will learn how all of this happens. Do you remember when we started this lesson, how that we asked if it was possible to depart from Christ? The child of God *falls* from grace when he *departs* from the living God. Therefore, "Beware, brethren, lest there be in any of you an evil heart of unbelief in departing from the living God; but exhort one another daily, while it is called 'Today,' lest any of you be hardened through the deceitfulness of sin. For we have become partakers of Christ if we hold the beginning of our confidence steadfast to the end..." (Hebrews 3:12-14).

The Savior teaches that no man is able "to pluck" us out of the Father's hand (John 10:28-29); but this is also conditioned upon our hearing His voice and following Him (John10:27). We have the promise that as long as we are hearing and following Christ we *"shall never perish."* It is when we quit hearing and following Christ that we depart from God.

By inspiration, Peter reminds us of this principle, "Therefore, brethren, be even more diligent to make your calling and election sure, for if you do these things you will never stumble; for so an entrance will be supplied to you abundantly into the everlasting kingdom of our Lord and Savior Jesus Christ" (2 Peter 1:10-11).

According to the Bible, Christians need to be diligent to make their calling and election sure by adding to our faith, that is, by growing in the grace and knowledge of the Lord

(2 Peter 3:18), and maturing in Christ as a manner of living. This is the manner of persons we ought to be (2 Peter 3:11-14). When we depart from the living God through the deceitfulness of sin, we must remember, repent, and return. "Remember therefore from where you have fallen; repent and do the first works" (Revelation 2:5). As James said, the erring child must be converted from the error of his ways.

CONCLUSION

It is God's will that we walk in His light, not in the darkness of sin. Please read 1 John 1:6-10 carefully with me. "If we say that we have fellowship with Him, and walk in darkness, we lie and do not practice the truth. But if we walk in the light as He is in the light, we have fellowship with one another, and the blood of Jesus Christ His Son cleanses us from all sin. If we say that we have no sin, we deceive ourselves, and the truth is not in us. If we confess our sins, He is faithful and just to forgive us our sins and to cleanse us from all unrighteousness. If we say that we have not sinned, we make Him a liar, and His word is not in us."

If we are in this condition, the apostle of God admonishes us to be honest about it. We have no reason to lie about it. A person cannot hide his sins from the all-seeing eye of God. If you say you have fellowship with Him and walk in darkness, you are living a life of deception. You lie and do not the truth. If we deny our sins, we make Him a liar and His word is not in us. Do you want this type of self-deception on your record when you appear at the final judgment?

Do as the prodigal son did. Repent, confess your sins, and ask God to forgive you. If you will do this, God says that He will forgive you and the blood of Christ will cleanse you of all unrighteousness. This is God's law of pardon for the erring Christian. He has a law of pardon for all those who have never obeyed the gospel and He has a law of pardon for those who have backslidden. Both are equally important.

Just as a lost soul must obey Christ and accept Him as Lord and Savior by repenting of sins and being baptized to wash them away (Acts 2:38), the erring child of God must acknowledge his sins, repent of them, and ask God to forgive Him. If either law of pardon applies to you, we hope you'll make the right decision and seek the help and forgiveness God is offering. He loves you. We all do. And we want to help you however we can.

THE PRODIGAL SON

In the fifteenth chapter of Luke, we read the parables of the lost sheep, the lost silver, and the lost son. The lost sheep signifies one who has become lost due to wandering. The lost silver illustrates someone lost due to the negligence of another. And the lost son depicts someone lost because of his "give me" mentality.

The lost sheep wandered aimlessly and, perhaps, for a period of time did not even realize he was lost, even as many wayward Christians often do. Slowly and gradually this sheep wandered far away from the fold, taking one step at a time. He needed a shepherd to go out and find him. Fortunately, he had such a Shepherd who was willing to sacrifice His time and energy to bring this lost sheep back into the fold. He left the ninety and nine to find the one. Upon finding the lost sheep, there was great rejoicing.

The silver was lost due to the carelessness of the woman. How many children are lost due to the carelessness of the parents! Perhaps she did not fully appreciate the coin's value until it had been lost to her. But, realizing the coin was lost, she swept and looked zealously until she found it. After finding the lost coin, she called her friends and neighbors together, saying, "Rejoice with me, for I have found the piece which I lost!"

The lost son is another story. He did not merely wander away from his father. He was not lost due to the carelessness of his father. He intentionally and willingly forsook his father's house. He wanted to leave. The lost son is the parable I am especially interested in presenting to you for this particular lesson. I am interested in his story because I believe he is a person with whom we can each relate. Perhaps some of us know a person who fits this young man's description well. Perhaps even one of us fits, or has fit, his description well.

"FATHER, GIVE ME"

Our Lord began this parable in Luke 15:11 by saying, "A certain man had two sons. And the younger of them said to his father, 'Father, give me the portion of goods that falls to me.' So he divided to them his livelihood." From the words, "give me" we find the root of the problem. This young son had a "give me" mentality. He was self-centered and self-serving. He was interested in himself, his wants, and his desires. He had greater plans (so he thought) than remaining at his father's house. He wanted to go and live his own life, free from his father's instruction and watchful eye. He was a young man who wanted to live for the moment. He wanted to live for the here-and-now. He wanted to bask in the riches and enjoy the fruits of his father's labor.

The "give me" mentality has long been the ruin of our society as well. Why do you suppose so many able-bodied people are on welfare in this country? Many of these people are guilty of wanting something for nothing. They have a "give me" mentality. They want everything given to them without having to pay the price of hard work to obtain.

Churches across this country are receiving countless calls for benevolent help because entire paychecks have been surrendered to the foolish lure of the lottery. Churches are unfairly asked to provide groceries, diapers, rent, and utility bills for people who have wasted their means upon the fantasy of winning big and never having to work again. What is the fascination with the lottery and the astronomical chances of winning? I submit to you it is the same "give me" mentality which drives the lottery as which drove the prodigal son away from his father's care.

Why do you suppose so many homes lay in ruin? If you will look closely, you will find that husband, wife, or both have digressed to a "give me" mentality. They are not interested in serving the other person or the best interests of their family; they are only worried about themselves, or their careers, or their prideful ambitions. Somewhere amongst all of this greed and selfishness is little "Johnny." And when the child begins to act out his frustrations at their neglect they respond by putting him in therapy and on medication, because, after all, something must be wrong with him.

Do you not know that the fastest growing market for antidepressants in this country is the preschoolers? At least four percent of all preschoolers – currently over one million – are clinically depressed. What is the cause of all this mayhem and madness in the home? We are living for the here-and-now. We are worldly and self-centered. We are demanding, "Give me!" and it has taken us into the distant country of sin and depression, far from our heavenly Father's care.

THE FAR COUNTRY

The "far country" of this parable does not represent a physical, geographical place, but a state of mind. When a person travels into this far country, he tends to separate himself from everything and everyone that would remind him of his heavenly Father. He begins by forsaking the assembly. He continues by severing all friendships with his brothers and sisters in the church. Before long, he is seldom seen or heard from in any setting that would include his brethren. He will even remove himself from the room when the conversation becomes too biblical in nature. I have even seen people in this state of mind leave the room before a prayer is said to bless the food!

The prodigal son wanted to be as far from his father as he could go. I ask you, what did his father do to deserve such treatment? He loved his son. He provided for his son. He cared for his son will the daily necessities of life – such as food, clothing, shelter, and safety.

What has God done that would warrant forsaking Him and His house? Has He not loved you? Has He not cared for you? Has He not kept you safely in the cleft of the rock and covered you with His hand (Exodus 33:22)?

THE MORNING OF DEPARTURE

A young man's "living" such as this parable represents in the ancient near eastern world would have included a vast sum of money and many sheep, oxen, camels, donkeys, chariots, possibly horses, and servants. The Lord tells us "And not many days after, the younger son gathered all together, journeyed to a far country."

What do you suppose the morning would have been like on the day the prodigal left home? Do you suppose he rose early, so that he could leave without confronting or seeing his father? Possibly, he was very careful as he quietly stirred around the house to dress, and pack, while preparing to leave. Possibly, his bags were already packed, as he had been preparing to leave for some time. Usually such decisions are not made on the spur of the moment.

Perhaps, there was a scene when this young man removed the signet ring of his father's family. This ring would have given him full privileges to his father's fortune for the purpose of buying and trading. It would have served as a seal of authority when its impression was placed on a document. I wonder what must have been going through his mind as he removed this ring from his finger.

Do you suppose he had any doubts, any second thoughts, as to the consequences of his decision and how his life was going to be changed? Do you suppose he left this ring somewhere he knew his father could find it – possibly a nightstand or on the bed? How do you suppose the father felt when he found his son's ring? What do you think went through his mind? Imagine how this father must have held on to that ring. I imagine he kept it in his pocket or somewhere on his person. Can you not see him sitting upon his porch, looking out over the horizon, gripping this ring in the palm of his hand, rubbing over its impressions with his fingers, wondering where his child must be?

The son's journey into the far country probably resembled a modern day parade or convoy. Can you not envision this young man heading this enormous caravan, his chest swelling with pride, his glare confident, his head held high, as the townspeople and villagers along the way would come out to line the roadside and see this great and important person pass? Don't you imagine they were thinking he was on his way to change the world and accomplish great things?

PRODIGAL LIVING

The Savior tells us upon his arrival into this distant country, possibly as far away from his father as he could get, he "wasted his possessions with prodigal (riotous, KJV) living." Sad words indeed.

He went off to conquer the world and achieve fame and greater fortune and all he accomplished was to *waste* his great inheritance and opportunity. He thought he could do better or have it better than he did at home. When we leave our Father's house, although we may think it is in our best interests, it simply amounts to a squandering of our great inheritance. We have an inheritance from God more precious than any earthly fortune. It is an inheritance which is incorruptible, undefiled, and does not fade away (1 Peter 1:4).

Things became worse for the young man far from home. Notice, "But when he had spent all, there arose a severe famine in that land, and he began to be in want." At one time, not too long ago, he had all his heart could desire and now he has nothing. Now he is in want. The good times have turned to despair. His so-called friends are gone and loneliness has set in.

Still, he has yet to learn his lesson. Rather than return home a failure and admit his wrong, the young man stubbornly took work. "Then he went and joined himself to a citizen of that country, and he sent him into his fields to feed swine."

Evidently his father did instill in him some work ethic. We do not leave every trace of our training and moorings when we leave the Father. Some life lessons leave indelible impressions which are not so easily erased.

How many people and places of employment do you suppose turned him down for him to accept *that* job? There was not a more demeaning work for a young Jewish man than feeding swine. Can you not picture him feeding those hogs? Can't you depict this once proud young man wearing dirty, torn, and tattered servant rags by that time? He probably sold all of his good clothes to continue his riotous living as long (at least) as he could hold out. If he was not wearing servant clothes, he was probably wearing the last of his custom sewn clothing, although by that time they were probably the equivalent of servant rags. We know that when he returned home, he was barefooted. Do you suppose he was barefooted out in those fields with the hogs?

Just picture him in your mind's eye. He's dirty. He needs to shave. His custom clothes are tattered and extremely filthy. He can't remember the last good meal he has enjoyed. He's desperate and alone.

ROCK BOTTOM

The Savior continues, "And he would gladly have filled his stomach with the pods that the swine ate, and no one gave him anything." This is what you call "rock bottom." Have you ever been that hungry? I can't say that I have. But now, no man will *give* unto him.

The "give me" mentality will only take you so far in life; and eventually *no man* will give unto you. Can't you see him asking for a handout? This once proud and dignified young man no longer has his head held high. His eyes no longer glare with confidence. The very people who lined the roadside to see his caravan pass are now witnessing the young man's appearance, smelling his odor, and laughing at his plea as he begs them for food and drink, *"and no one gave him anything."*

I am reminded of the question Paul asked his brethren at Rome, "What fruit had ye then in those things whereof now ye are ashamed? For the end of those things is death?" This young man's journey away from his father has proven to be fruitless. He has found himself in a rut; and it's going to take his father to pull him out of this rut.

When we find ourselves in this condition spiritually, know this, it is going to take our heavenly Father to pull us out. Just as the young man could not have his life restored without returning to his father, loved one, you cannot have your soul restored without returning to your Father.

Thankfully, we can go home again! I am reminded of how God pleaded with the children of Israel and Judah, "Return to Me" (Jeremiah 3:1, 7), but they would not.

Is God not also now longing to see all of His prodigal children return to Him? He considers our souls to be the most precious possessions of the earth. He is engaged in the greatest of conflicts with the forces of darkness to save our souls. He believes our souls to be so valuable that He was willing to give the ransom of His Son – the highest ransom He could pay – to redeem us from sin. How can any man choose to perish in the far country of sin, when we have a Father who is so good to us and is willing to forgive us and welcome us home?

WAKE UP, GET UP, AND FESS UP

Our Lord continues, "But when he came to himself, he said, 'How many of my father's hired servants have bread enough and to spare, and I perish with hunger!'" *"And when he came to himself"* – this is the key moment of change for the good in this young man's life. He had to wake up! He had to snap out of it.

How many times do you suppose he starred at the reflection of his tired, bloodshot eyes and did nothing? But this time he sees those same empty eyes looking back at him and he is no longer satisfied. The satisfaction from sinful living will only last for so long.

Moses chose "to suffer affliction with the people of God, than to enjoy the pleasures of sin *for a season*." The pleasures of sin are only for a season. The good times will run out, and when they do, so too will all the good time friends you thought you gained along the way.

Let me ask you, where were all these people who helped him live riotously in that distant land when *he* was in need?

100

Do you really think that kind of person is going to be there for you when *you* are in need? This time the young man looked into the depths of those bloodshot eyes and saw himself as he really was, a pathetic, self-centered, selfish, spoiled child who squandered every good thing he had and trampled beneath his feet every person who ever loved him.

He decided, "I will arise and go to my father, and will say to him, "Father, I have sinned against heaven and before you, and I am no longer worthy to be called your son. Make me like one of your hired servants." It's not enough to wake up. You have to get up. And, you have to 'fess up.

Many of our erring brethren *know* they are in error and yet will refuse to do something about. They have to do something about it! It profits them nothing to remain in that condition. They're still in that far country, and that's not going to change, until they do something about it.

Sure, you can be dissatisfied and you can even realize where your sins have taken you, but until you do something about it, you will remain in your sins and separated from God. The lost son was going to do something about his condition. He wasn't satisfied to keep living the way he was. He wanted something better out of life. He knew there was a better life out there to be enjoyed. He knew that life even as a servant of his father's house was better than his present situation.

"And he arose, and came to his father." This is what an erring child of God must do today. You must come to your heavenly Father.

A HAPPY REUNION

If you have ever wondered how God would receive you upon this decision, just read what happens next. "But when he was still a great way off, his father saw him and had

101

compassion, and ran and fell on his neck and kissed him. And the son said to him, 'Father, I have sinned against heaven and in your sight, and am no longer worthy to be called your son.' But the father said to his servants, 'Bring out the best robe and put it on him, and put a ring on his hand and sandals on his feet. And bring the fatted calf here and kill it, and let us eat and be merry; for this my son was dead and is alive again; he was lost and is found.' And they began to be merry."

I want you to see that his father did not shame him. He happily welcomed his son home. The father did not begrudge the son. He restored his son to the family and all its treasures. The son's ring was restored to him. Upon seeing and embracing his son, he did not give him a trial period to see if he was sincere. He restored him immediately to his house, just as he was before, just as if none of this had ever happened.

The same scene can be replayed and revisited now, if the erring child will come home. If you will arise and go to your heavenly Father and confess your sins and ask for His forgiveness, He is faithful and just to forgive your sins and cleanse you from all unrighteousness. But you have to come home.

You're going to have to do it. I wish you'd do it. Your brothers and sisters in Christ want to see you restored. The angels are watching. Your Savior is waiting. Your Father is standing a long way off, looking into the distance, hoping to see that one, lone silhouette emerging over that vast horizon. He will run to meet you. He will forgive you and restore your inheritance. Will you not come? Come home now.

THE MOST MISUNDERSTOOD PAGE IN THE BIBLE

In most Bibles you will find a leaflet of paper separating the Old and New Testaments. It has been claimed that the only difference between the Old and New Testaments is this little leaflet of paper. For obvious reasons which we shall study in this lesson, this little leaflet of paper has become for many the most misunderstood page in the Bible.

FAILURE TO UNDERSTAND
THE RECIPIENTS OF THE LAW

This page is misunderstood because of a failure to recognize that the Bible contains two different covenants which God made with two different people. The Old Testament is the covenant law given to Israel because of their transgressions in the wilderness (Galatians 3:19). The old law served as a schoolmaster or tutor to bring them (Israel) to the system of faith which is the law of Christ (Galatians 3:24) – God's eternal purpose and covenant (Ephesians 3:10-11).

The New Testament is the covenant law that is now effectual for "every tribe and tongue, people and nation" (Revelation 5:9). God promises those who are in this new covenant: "I will be merciful to their unrighteousness, and their sins and their lawless deeds I will remember no more" (Hebrews 8:12). The new covenant, the law of Christ, is the only covenant God has ever made with man in which He has attached this promise of complete forgiveness and no more remembrance of sins. According to the old covenant, God would "visit the iniquity of the fathers upon the children and the children's children unto the third and fourth generation" (Exodus 34:7).

Christians, however, have no continual burnt, meal, sin, peace, or trespass offerings. There is no annual Day of

Atonement. We have the blood of Christ – *"one sacrifice for sins forever"* (Hebrews 10:12). God promises His people if we will "walk in the light as He is in the light, we have fellowship with one another, and the blood of Jesus Christ His Son cleanses us from all sin" (1 John 1:7).

The writer of Hebrews comments: "In that He says, 'A new covenant,' He has made the first obsolete" ("old," KJV). Now what is becoming obsolete and growing old is ready to vanish away" (Hebrews 8:13).

It is good for us to know why we call the Old Testament *"old."* God made this covenant "old" when He established the *"new."* "He takes away the first that He may establish the second" (Hebrews 10:9). We now have "a better covenant, which was established on better promises" (Hebrews 8:6).

The law of Moses was given specifically to the nation of Israel and none other. When God spoke with Moses in the mountain top of Sinai, He said that His word was to be directed unto "the house of Jacob and the children of Israel" (Exodus 19:3, 5-6). God also spoke to Israel through Jeremiah when the time came to inform them of a new covenant (Jeremiah 31:34). Such information would be pointless if

That God never intended for that law to serve as His universal covenant for the Christian faith is further proven by Paul's statement in Romans 3:19. He wrote, "Now we know that whatever the law says, it says to those who are under the law, that every mouth may be stopped, and all the world may become guilty before God."

A law only speaks to those who are under it. The law of Moses never spoke to any other nation, including the church. The law was to be preached unto Israel just as the gospel is to be preached unto every creature and nation today. Christ said, "preach the gospel unto every creature" (Mark 16:15), and "teach all nations" (Matthew 28:18-20). These are two different religious systems for two different groups of people. One system has ceased and the other system is now in place.

Jesus Christ gave the gospel, the new covenant, as a spiritual law to speak to every nation, people, kindred, and tongue of the earth. The gospel, not the law of Moses, has been ordained by God to be the universal covenant between God and man. Just as Israel was peculiar (special) to God in that system, Christians are peculiar (special) to God in the gospel system (1 Peter 2:9).

FAILURE TO UNDERSTAND THE PURPOSE OF THE LAW

The law was given to Israel because of Israel's transgressions in the wilderness. Listen to what Paul said in Galatians 3:19: "What purpose then does the law serve? It was added because of transgressions, till the Seed should come to whom the promise was made; and it was appointed through angels by the hand of a mediator."

The law served as a means of teaching and keeping Abraham's descendants holy until the promise made in Genesis 12:3 would be fulfilled in Christ. You see, Israel was greatly blessed to have all of those wonderful prophets preaching unto them and the watchful eye of a loving God upon them. This is the meaning of Paul's statement in Romans 3:1-2. Paul asked, "What advantage then has the Jew, or what is the profit of circumcision? Much in every way! Chiefly because to them were committed the oracles of God."

Israel had the word of God directing their steps, serving as their moral and civil law, to bring them unto the Christ and His gospel. It was given to serve as a schoolmaster, or tutor, to Israel to bring them to faith in Christ, that they

105

might be justified by faith (Galatians 3:24). The "school-master" was responsible for bringing the child to the teacher. This was the purpose of the law to Israel. The law was intended to bring the child (Israel) to the Teacher (Christ).

Paul adds, "But after faith has come, we are no longer under a tutor" (v.25). In the eyes of God, in the Christian age, "There is neither Jew nor Greek, there is neither slave nor free, there is neither male nor female; for you are all one in Christ Jesus. And if you are Christ's, then you are Abraham's seed, and heirs according to the promise" (Galatians 3:28-29).

God kept His promise in Christ and all nations of the earth are blessed by the Seed of Abraham who died for the sin of the world. God's intention from the beginning, as seen in His promise to Abraham, was to bless every nation with the opportunity of salvation and a covenant relationship with Him, thus bringing the faithful of every nation to faith in Christ Jesus.

For Christians, the law is intended to be used for our learning (Romans 15:4). From it we learn more of God, His character, and His dealings with man. And, "all these things happened to them as examples, and they were written for our admonition, on whom the ends of the ages have come. Therefore let him who thinks he stands take heed lest he fall" (1 Corinthians 10:11-12).

We have many lessons to learn from the Old Testament, but the words of Christ, and not Moses, are for our keeping. Even Moses said of Christ, "The Lord your God will raise up for you a Prophet like me from your midst, from your brethren. Him you shall hear..." (Deuteronomy 18:15). Moses was telling Israel that the time was going to come when they would have to stop living by that law and begin living by the law of Christ.

The law was never able to cleanse the conscience as it was never able to take away sins. There was always a remembrance of sin under the law. The writer of Hebrews wrote of this very thing when he said: "For the law, having a shadow of the good things to come, and not the very image of the things, can never with these same sacrifices, which they offer continually year by year, make those who approach perfect. For then would they not have ceased to be offered? For the worshipers, once purged, would have had no more consciousness of sins. But in those sacrifices there is a reminder of sins every year. For it is not possible that the blood of bulls and goats could take away sins" (Hebrews 10:1-4).

Not even the most faithful under the law of Moses were cleansed by those offerings. These dear souls were, however, ultimately forgiven by the blood of Christ. Note: "...being justified freely by His grace through the redemption that is in Christ Jesus, whom God set forth to be a propitiation by His blood, through faith, to demonstrate His righteousness, because in His forbearance, God had passed over the sins that were previously committed, to demonstrate at the present time His righteousness, that He might be just and the justifier of the one who has faith in Jesus" (Romans 3:24-26).

Read again with me from the writer of Hebrews: "And for this reason He is the Mediator of the new covenant, by means of death, for the redemption of the transgressions under the first covenant, that those who are called may receive the promise of the eternal inheritance" (Hebrews 9:15).

The blood of Christ was shed for the redemption of all the faithful under the first covenant as well as all the faithful under the new covenant. No soul can be saved from sin, in any age, except by the blood of Christ.

107

"By that will we have been sanctified through the offering of the body of Jesus Christ once for all. And every priest stands ministering daily and offering repeatedly the same sacrifices, which can never take away sins. But this Man, after He had offered one sacrifice for sins forever, sat down at the right hand of God..." (Hebrews 10:10-12).

FAILURE TO UNDERSTAND THE DURATION OF THE LAW

God made it clear through Jeremiah that He would establish a new covenant (Jeremiah 31:31-34). Furthermore, on at least two occasions, when contrasted with Moses, we are told to "hear" or "listen to" Christ (Deuteronomy 18:15; Matthew 17:5).

Christ fulfilled the law of Moses and nailed it to His cross. However, to those Jews who died under the law, it was eternally significant. By that law their faithfulness to God was and ultimately will be judged. "For as many as have sinned without law will also perish without law, and as many as have sinned in the law will be judged by the law" (Romans 2:12).

At times in the Old Testament, you will find the law described as an "everlasting" covenant or statute with Israel; and to those Jews who lived then, who shall be judged by it, it is as everlasting as the gospel is to us. On the Judgment Day, the books of the Old Testament will read exactly the same to the Jew who lived thereby as the books of the New Testament will read to those of this age.

It is important that we understand that Moses was speaking to Jews under that law and of that age before Christ when he referred to the law as "everlasting." While the law will judge those Israelites of that era, it can never justify them.

According to Paul "no one is justified by the law in the sight of God is evident, for 'The just shall live by faith.' Yet the law is not of faith, but 'The man who does them shall live by them.' Christ has redeemed us from the curse of the law, having become a curse for us (for it is written, 'Cursed is everyone who hangs on a tree'), that the blessing of Abraham might come upon the Gentiles in Christ Jesus, that we might receive the promise of the Spirit through faith" (Galatians 3:11-14).

In Galatians 3, Paul provides an overview of God's dealings with the children of Abraham. God made a promise to Abraham that from his seed all the nations of the earth would be blessed. The law, that came four hundred years after this promise, could not disannul the fact that all nations of the earth (the Gentiles) would be blessed.

The law was added because of Israel's transgressions, to serve as a tutor, to bring them unto the time of Christ. The law offered life to anyone who could keep it perfectly, but no man could, save one – Jesus Christ. Thus, the law became a curse to the Jews because of their failure to keep it perfectly and thus find justification therein. But Christ, who kept it perfectly, took the curse of the law away by His sacrifice for our sins, "hanging on the tree," bringing redemption and justification for the sins the law could not touch.

FAILURE TO UNDERSTAND
THE FULFILLMENT OF THE LAW

Christ came to fulfill the law (Matthew 5:17-18). The door of opportunity for a covenant with all people has been opened. Christ established His kingdom in which His law governs and His grace forgives.

Paul writes: "Therefore remember that you, once Gentiles in the flesh who are called Uncircumcision by what is called the Circumcision made in the flesh by hands that at that time you were without Christ, being aliens from the commonwealth of Israel and strangers from the covenants of promise, having no hope and without God in the world. But now in Christ Jesus you who once were far off have been made near by the blood of Christ. For He Himself is our peace, Who has made both one, and has broken down the middle wall of division between us, having abolished in His flesh the enmity, that is, the law of commandments contained in ordinances, so as to create in Himself one new man from the two, thus making peace, and that He might reconcile them both to God in one body through the cross, thereby putting to death the enmity" (Ephesians 2:11-16).

To make the law binding on men today is to leave anyone but a Jew outside the doors of fellowship with God. Moreover, it is to leave the Jew under the curse of the law without any possibility of ultimate forgiveness.

We don't have to worry about such dark and grim circumstances because the Bible teaches us that the law has been nailed to the cross (Colossians 2:14) – including ceremonial laws such as the Sabbath (Colossians 2:17).

By His death and the coming of the New Testament, Christ made the Old Testament "old" (Hebrews 8:13). Christ took away the first so that He could establish the second (Hebrews 10:9). God caused the Law of Moses "to be done away...abolished...in Christ" (2 Corinthians 3:6-18).

Christ is now the High Priest over the house of God (Hebrews 4:4-16), which is the household of faith (Galatians 6:10). "For the priesthood being changed, of necessity there is also a change of the law" (Hebrews 7:12).

CONCLUSION

The law was limited in its recipients, its purpose, and its duration. The law could not perfect the conscience (Hebrews 9:9), because it could never fully satisfy our sin debt (Hebrews 10:1). We now have a better covenant, which has been established on better promises (Hebrews 8:6-7).

Man is now saved by the gospel (Romans 1:16-17). God has promised and given a new covenant (Hebrews 8:8-12). Man must now obey the gospel of Christ – not the Law of Moses – if he is to be saved.

Indeed, something much greater than a leaflet of paper stands between these two covenants. The cross of Christ stands between them! We invite you to come to the cross, obey the gospel, and wash every sin way.

YOUTH FOR CHRIST

"Rejoice, O young man, in your youth, And let your heart cheer you in the days of your youth; Walk in the ways of your heart, And in the sight of your eyes; But know that for all these God will bring you into judgment. Therefore remove sorrow from your heart, And put away evil from your flesh, For childhood and youth are vanity. Remember now your Creator in the days of your youth, Before the difficult days come, And the years draw near when you say, 'I have no pleasure in them'" (Ecclesiastes 11:9-12:1).

Concerned souls stand watching and waiting to see what this generation will do with the days of their youth. Elderly Christians who have "fought the good fight" are especially concerned to know the things their children and grandchildren will do with the days of youth. They simply want to be assured that they are preparing for the "difficult days" to come.

The days of youth are so very important because it is the time that we have to study and prepare for the opportunities and challenges of tomorrow. Knowing this, President Lincoln once said, "I will study and prepare, and perhaps someday my chance will come."

During the days of youth, children are trained in the way they should go (Proverbs 22:6). Parents must not neglect this responsibility. Rather, they must treat their children as gifts from God. "Behold, children are a heritage from the Lord, The fruit of the womb is His reward. Like arrows in the hand of a warrior, So are the children of one's youth" (Psalm 127:3-4).

William Wordsworth keenly observed, "The child is father of the man." Indeed, the qualities, virtues, characteristics, and values we learn as children will eventually mold us into the adults we become.

As we discuss the theme of "Youth for Christ," I would especially like for young people to pay close attention, but I would also like for the parents and grandparents to pay close attention to the things we shall study. Everyone can contribute to the future of the Lord's church. Just as Moses was eighty years old when God called on him to be a spiritual leader to His people, who is to say that God will not call on you to do likewise today?

Young Christians and young Christian families must be challenged to greater faithfulness and obedience in the Lord. I know of no better way to challenge young and old alike than by looking into the mirror of the soul that is the word of God. "How can a young man cleanse his way? By taking heed according to Your word" (Psalm 119:9).

Let us look to the Bible and ask three decisive questions of our youth: Are you willing to sacrifice for the Lord? Are you willing to serve the Lord? And, are you willing to stand for the Lord? As we discuss these questions, I would like for brethren of each generation present to ask what they are doing to encourage and help their young brethren and children to be faithful in this generation.

ARE YOU WILLING TO SACRIFICE FOR THE LORD?

Young man, young woman, are you willing to sacrifice for the Lord? Take for example the actions of the rich young ruler (Luke 18:18-23). Here was a young man with a legitimate concern. He asked Christ, "Good Teacher, what shall I do to inherit eternal life?" This is a question young people everywhere should be asking.

Jesus said to him, "Why do you call Me good? No one is good but One, that is, God. You know the commandments:

'Do not commit adultery,' 'Do not murder,' 'Do not steal,' 'Do not bear false witness,' 'Honor your father and your mother.'"

You will observe that Jesus did not preach the "faith only" doctrine. Also note the very good life that the young man had lived to that point. He said, "All these things I have kept from my youth." We can appreciate several things which were highly commendable about this young man. He came asking the right question. He went to the right Person to find the answer. He knew Jesus was the One to ask. And obviously, he had been faithful to God in many regards. Yet, his willingness to serve Christ would be challenged with Christ's reply.

Jesus answered him by saying, "You still lack one thing. Sell all that you have and distribute to the poor, and you will have treasure in heaven; and come, follow Me." Matthew's account includes the phrase, "If you would be perfect..." The idea is that of being completely submissive to the will of God. Evidently, this young man's riches were keeping him from being completely submissive to God, and for this we cannot commend him.

You will note that "when he heard this, he became very sorrowful, for he was very rich." He was as sorry as he was rich. Here was a young man who could have walked in the very footsteps of Christ, but rather than rejoice, he felt full of sorrow. He would not give up his riches in order to obey the Lord. When it came to his riches, his was not willing to sacrifice so that he could follow Christ. I do not know whatever became of this young man, but I do know that his unwillingness to sacrifice the corruptible riches of this life caused him to miss out on the unsearchable riches that would have come by following the Savior.

Also consider the example of Saul of Tarsus. Saul was a rising star among the Jews. When Saul was a young man, he held the garments for those who stoned Stephen (Acts 7:58).

As a young man, he devoted his life to learning the law of God. Concerning his raising, Paul wrote that he was, "circumcised the eighth day, of the stock of Israel, of the tribe of Benjamin, a Hebrew of the Hebrews; concerning the law, a Pharisee; concerning zeal, persecuting the church; concerning the righteousness which is in the law, blameless" (Philippians 3:5-6).

He was educated at the feet of Gamaliel (Acts 22:3) and was certainly esteemed among the Pharisees. It could be that someday he might have gained the prominence of his teacher and possibly could have sat on the Jewish High Council, the Sanhedrin.

However, having learned the truth, Paul could truthfully write of himself, "what things were gain to me, these I have counted loss for Christ" (Philippians 3:7). Wouldn't it be wonderful if every one of us could truthfully say the same of ourselves!

How much stronger do you suppose we could make the church? How many more souls do you suppose we could save? How much stronger would our community and family be because of the decision to count all things loss for Christ? Paul was willing to sacrifice all earthly wealth and fame to follow his Lord. He epitomized the thought of seeking first the kingdom. He was crucified to the world and crucified with Christ.

I believe you'll also find the example of Moses' youth to be worth considering. Moses chose to live as a child of God rather than a child of Pharaoh.

"By faith Moses, when he became of age, refused to be called the son of Pharaoh's daughter, choosing rather to suffer affliction with the people of God than to enjoy the passing pleasures of sin, esteeming the reproach of Christ greater riches than the treasures in Egypt; for he looked to the reward" (Hebrews 11:24-26).

He realized the pleasure of sin was only for a season, but the reward of faith was for all eternity. Young Christians must avoid being allured and deceived by the pleasures of sin. Sin is in abundance. Sin is everywhere. And while we may have to live in a world full of sinful temptations for a time, we must never become "of the world" and yield to these evil things.

"Do not love the world or the things in the world. If anyone loves the world, the love of the Father is not in him. For all that is in the world—the lust of the flesh, the lust of the eyes, and the pride of life—is not of the Father but is of the world. And the world is passing away, and the lust of it; but he who does the will of God abides forever" (1 John 2:15-17).

Young people must have their priorities in order. "Flee youthful lusts..." (2 Timothy 2:22). Being young is no excuse to disobey God.

Paul and Moses were willing to sacrifice for the Lord. The rich young ruler was unwilling to sacrifice for the Lord. Paul and Moses realized a great purpose to life and enjoyed the bliss that comes from being in the happy care of Providence. The rich young ruler was full of sorrow. Young man, young woman, are you willing to sacrifice for the Lord? Are you willing to forsake earthly friendships which would tempt you to sin? Are you willing to walk away from a boyfriend or girlfriend because of their unwillingness to obey the Lord? Are you willing to sacrifice the notion of

117

popularity and being one of the "cool kids" because you realize drunkenness, drugs, and fornication are sinful? Paul once asked, "What fruit did you have in those things whereof now you are ashamed?" (Romans 6:21) If you are unwilling to make these sacrifices for the Lord, someday you will look back upon the days of your youth with shame.

ARE YOU WILLING TO SERVE THE LORD?

Young Christians must also learn to work for the Lord while they are young. They should be found taking an active and involved interest in the work of the church. As they grow, their abilities, usefulness, and responsibilities should likewise grow. Youth man, young woman, are you willing to work for the Lord?

To illustrate, let us look at Timothy's example. Timothy came from a good home with a Christian mother and grandmother, although his father was a Greek (2 Timothy 1:5; Acts 16:1). He was converted on the first missionary journey and by the time of the second missionary journey, he was converting others. He was admonished by Paul, "Let no man despise thy youth" (1 Timothy 4:12).

The only way a young person can accomplish this is to have moral character that is worthy of respect. Paul continues, "...but be an example to the believers in word, in conduct, in love, in spirit, in faith, in purity." If you have this type of a solid foundation, built upon biblically principled morals, you will have something worthy of respect.

Consider also Mark's example. He too came from a good home. His mother appears to have been a fine Christian lady (see Acts 12:12), and Barnabas (his uncle) must have been a good influence on young Mark.

Mark was given a great opportunity at a very young age to accompany Paul and Barnabas on the first missionary journey (Acts 11:25). Yet, time would prove that he was not yet ready, as he returned home (Acts 13:13).

However, Mark *became* ready. So much so that the last words we have of Paul pertaining to Mark read thusly: "Get Mark and bring him with you, for he is useful to me for ministry" (2 Timothy 4:11). It is not where you start, but where you finish!

What a wonderful compliment to say of any person, but especially of a young person – he is useful to me for ministry! A wonderful goal for the days of youth is to be useful for the ministry.

ARE YOU WILLING TO STAND FOR THE LORD?

Young people must also be found standing for the Lord. I cannot help but be reminded of David's example while facing the formidable giant Goliath (1 Samuel 17:1-54). Do you recall how he could not tolerate the enemy's taunts? The enemy Goliath was mocking God and this caused young David to wonder why no one had stopped him. He asked, "Who is this uncircumcised Philistine, that should defy the armies of the living God?" David realized someone had to do something and he chose to be that someone.

I believe we each can appreciate the fact that David did not stop at words. He had prepared himself. His trust was in the Lord. And, he was willing to give God all the glory. In contrast, also observe the example of David's brother, Eliab. The Bible reads, "Now Eliab his oldest brother heard when he spoke to the men; and Eliab's anger was aroused against David, and he said, 'Why did you come down here? And with whom have you left those few sheep in the wilderness? I know your pride and the insolence of your heart, for you have come down to see the battle'" (1 Samuel 17:28).

Eliab had also heard the taunting of Goliath and he likewise had the chance to make a stand, but he chose to do nothing. It seems that he was angry because David did not share in his fear. He accused David wrongfully instead of recognizing the cause. David answered, "What have I done now? Is there not a cause?" (1 Samuel 17:29)

Brethren, sometimes we need a young person to ask us, "Is there not a cause?" Sometimes we need to be reminded of the cause. We live in a world filled with enemies of the cross. Shall we follow David's example and stand for the Lord? Or, shall we follow Eliab's example and seek to criticize and jealously discourage anyone who would dare stand?

Not only did David face his brother's criticism, but he also faced his king's doubts. Saul observed, "You are not able to go against this Philistine to fight with him; for you are a youth, and he a man of war from his youth" (1 Samuel 17:33). Saul was underestimating a young person who was willing and prepared to stand for his God!

David spoke the understanding of his heart when he answered, "The LORD, who delivered me from the paw of the lion and from the paw of the bear, He will deliver me from the hand of this Philistine" (1 Samuel 17:37). God can and will deliver each of us if we will put our trust in him and obey His word. "What shall we say then to these things, if God be for us, who can be against us?" (Romans 8:31)

Young man, young woman, do you recognize the cause? Are you willing to stand for the cause of the Lord? Will you stand for His cause when the gospel is opposed? Will you stand for His cause when God's mission is opposed? Will you stand for Jesus, when His morality is opposed? Truly, these are questions for every generation, congregation, household, and individual. Let each one determine to stand fast in the faith!

CONCLUSION

By way of conclusion, I would like to take you back to Ecclesiastes 11:9-12. This is where we began this lesson. Now let us conclude by noting some things we should know about the days of youth.

First of all, young Christians and young people of an age of accountability need to know that they are responsible to God for the decisions they make. "God will bring you into judgment" (Ecclesiastes 11:9). You can follow those things that allure the eyes and tempt the soul, but know that God will judge young and old alike for their decisions.

Secondly, put away sorrow and evil in the days of youth, and learn about God. Learning of the God who created you and loves you dearly will give you a solid foundation for this life and the life to come. Difficult days will come and you will need to have the right mentality of faith and conviction to deal with such things. Learn of God's will *before* these days come and you will be better prepared to deal with them *when* they come.

"Therefore remove sorrow from your heart, And put away evil from your flesh, For childhood and youth are vanity. Remember now your Creator in the days of your youth, Before the difficult days come, And the years draw near when you say, 'I have no pleasure in them'" (Ecclesiastes 11:10-12:1).

Someday your spirit will return to God and you will reap what you have sown (Ecclesiastes 12:7). You must prepare for that day. "Remember thy Creator in the days of thy youth..." Whether young or old, we must learn to "Fear God and keep His commandments" (Ecclesiastes 12:13); for, "God will bring every work to judgment and every secret thing whether it is good or whether it is evil" (Ecclesiastes 12:14).

Young man, young woman, are you willing to sacrifice for the Lord? Will you serve Him? Are you prepared to stand for Him? Why not give God your heart and life now, while you are young? Don't shortchange Him. Don't wait until you're a dying man to get religion. You may not get the chance. Don't wait until after you have chosen a spouse and raised a family before you decide to seek the Lord. You will not be doing them the kind of good you could do them by obeying Christ in the days of your youth and serving Him faithfully throughout your life.

The most successful strategy for life is to make things right with God *first* and then build your life on that solid foundation of faithfulness. We invite you to build your life upon the Rock of ages by obeying the everlasting gospel of our Lord.

THE CHURCH IN THE MYSTERY OF THE AGES

God determined the last day of His creation, even before giving dawn's light to the first day. God's works were finished from the foundation of the world (Hebrews 4:3); and He included a plan to save me.

God has also appointed a day in which "He will judge the world in righteousness by the Man Whom He has ordained. He has given assurance of this to all by raising Him from the dead" (Acts 17:31).

God will judge the world in righteousness by His Son, Jesus Christ. "The Lord knows how to deliver the godly out of temptations and to reserve the unjust under punishment for the day of judgment, and especially those who walk according to the flesh in the lust of uncleanness and despise authority" (2 Peter 2:9-10). The saved, however, "according to His promise, look for new heavens and a new earth in which righteousness dwells" (2 Peter 3:13).

God determined a plan to save man before man ever sinned, even before man was ever created. God, knowing His creation would sin against Him, determined aforetime to send His only begotten Son in the form of man, to die as a man and to be resurrected, in order to reconcile the sinful unto the Righteous. Jesus Christ is the Lamb of God was "slain from the foundation of the world" (Revelation 13:8).

Peter wrote, "He indeed was foreordained before the foundation of the world, but was manifest in these last times for you who through Him believe in God, who raised Him from the dead and gave Him glory, so that your faith and hope are in God" (1 Peter 1:20-21).

It was before the foundation of the world that God determined for His Son to establish a kingdom never to be destroyed, to begin upon this earth, and ultimately to be gathered to its eternal home in the heavens. Someday Jesus will say to His church, "Come, you blessed of My Father, inherit the kingdom prepared for you from the foundation of the world" (Matthew 25:34).

We know not of one aspect of the kingdom which is a matter merely of happenstance. God has acted deliberately in every way imaginable to man to show man that His kingdom is here for a reason – an eternal purpose – so that "the manifold wisdom of God might be made known by the church to the principalities and powers in the heavenly places, according to the eternal purpose which He accomplished in Christ Jesus our Lord" (Ephesians 3:10-11).

Every aspect of the Christian religion is a matter of divine revelation and authority. It is not a mistake, a result of haphazard, last minute planning, or human innovation that we speak of the churches of Christ (Romans 16:16).

It is because of God's infinite wisdom and eternal purpose to save man, that He calls us out of the darkness of ignorance and sin, and gathers us together into a spiritual body of believers with His only Son, seated as Head with all power and authority.

What we intend to teach in this lesson is the fact that the church has existed all along. It has existed in the mind of God, in the mystery of the ages.

The word "mystery" in the New Testament denotes a subject or prophecy of old which needed further revelation or fulfillment in order for us as Christians to have a correct understanding. Prior to such revelation, the subject's full meaning was "hidden" in the sense that complete understanding was not yet attained on the part of the hearer.

The idea behind the word "mystery" is as a general that is executing his battle strategy. The general's strategy has been hidden, not yet fully revealed, until the time of execution.

Of the eternal strategy of God, Paul wrote, "But we speak the wisdom of God in a mystery, the hidden wisdom which God ordained before the ages for our glory, which none of the rulers of this age knew; for had they known, they would not have crucified the Lord of glory" (1 Corinthians 2:7-8).

Paul also spoke authoritatively pertaining to his role and the role of the apostles saying, "Let a man so consider us, as servants of Christ and stewards of the mysteries of God" (1 Corinthians 4:1). The "mysteries of God" were the things which God had not revealed fully in the Old Testament, but was fulfilling through Paul and the other apostles.

Of this "mystery" Paul also said, "in other ages was not made known to the sons of men, as it has now been revealed by the Spirit to His holy apostles and prophets" (Ephesians 3:5).

Matthew wrote of Jesus' use of parables by quoting Psalms 78:2, "I will open My mouth in parables; I will utter things which have been kept secret from the foundation of the world" (Matthew 13:35).

Peter wrote, "Of this salvation the prophets have inquired and searched diligently, who prophesied of the grace that would come to you, searching what, or what manner of time, the Spirit of Christ who was in them was indicating when He testified beforehand the sufferings of Christ and the glories that would follow. To them it was revealed that, not to themselves, but to us they were ministering the things which now have been reported to you through those who have preached the gospel to you by the Holy Spirit sent from heaven things which angels desire to look into" (1 Peter 1:10-12).

125

Peter understood that these Old Testament writers were writing by the inspiration of the Holy Spirit, for, "no prophecy of Scripture is of any private interpretation, for prophecy never came by the will of man, but holy men of God spoke as they were moved by the Holy Spirit" (2 Peter 1:20-21). He also understood that he had a very special place in the divine plan of redemption. He was communicating the answers to the prophecies for which the Old Testament heroes could only "desire to look into."

Of the relationship between Old Testament prophecy and New Testament fulfillment, especially concerning Christ and His kingdom, Peter would say publicly to Jews at Jerusalem: "For Moses truly said to the fathers, 'The Lord your God will raise up for you a Prophet like me from your brethren. Him you shall hear in all things, whatever He says to you. And it shall come to pass that every soul who will not hear that Prophet shall be utterly destroyed from among the people.' Yes, and all the prophets, from Samuel and those who follow, as many as have spoken, have also foretold these days" (Acts 3:22-24).

THE CHRIST IN THE MYSTERY OF THE AGES

If we take these Old Testament prophecies concerning the kingdom, and ignore their New Testament explanations, we will abide in darkness and continue to grope in darkness seeking and yet gaining no correct understanding. We must live by that old adage, "The New Testament reveals what the Old Testament conceals."

Moreover, when the New Testament provides an explanation to an Old Testament prophecy we ought to respect it as the intended purpose and fulfillment of that prophecy. In other words, when we read, "This is that which was spoken by the prophet..." we ought not to be found saying, "But it

126

could also mean..." God has given us the explanation by divine revelation and that should suffice.

With this fundamental principle of Bible interpretation in mind, let us go all the way back to the first Messianic prophecy revealed in scripture, Genesis 3:15. From this passage we learn that the seed of woman would someday crush the head of Satan. From Genesis 12:3, we learn this seed would come through the family of Abraham. From Isaiah 7:14, we learn the woman from Abraham's family that would beget this Child would be a virgin. And, from Isaiah 53 we learn that the purpose of this Child would be to make intercession for transgressors.

Now, just on the basis of the Old Testament, one is left wondering who this person would be. Those who claim to be Jews today are still wondering. They abide in disbelief because they have failed to accept the revelation of the New Testament. But, when we turn to the New Testament, all of these prophetical queries are answered after reading only the *first chapter*. Isn't that amazing! The Bible is an amazing book.

Just turn to Matthew chapter one and read the angelic utterance given to Joseph concerning the baby in the womb of his virgin soon-to-be wife: "Joseph, son of David, do not be afraid to take to you Mary your wife, for that which is conceived in her is of the Holy Spirit. And she will bring forth a Son, and you shall call His name Jesus, for He will save His people from their sins." Matthew then explains, "Now all this was done that it might be fulfilled which was spoken by the Lord through the prophet, saying: 'Behold, a virgin shall be with child, and bear a Son, and they shall call His name Immanuel,' which is translated, 'God with us'" (Matthew 1:20-23).

127

The angel was speaking of the "mystery of godliness" according to 1Timothy 3:16. Note, "And without controversy great is the mystery of godliness: God was manifested in the flesh, justified in the Spirit, seen by angels, preached among the Gentiles, believed on in the world, received up in glory."

Paul was writing about the Christ. Christ's coming into the world was "the mystery of godliness." He was God manifested in the flesh. He was "God with us" – *that it might be fulfilled.*

As Isaiah said, "For unto us a Child is born, unto us a Son is given; and the government will be upon His shoulder. And His name will be called Wonderful, Counselor, Mighty God, Everlasting Father, Prince of Peace" (Isaiah 9:6).

For us to understand the work of Christ in God's eternal purpose, one must accept the New Testament's explanations of these Old Testament prophecies. God had a plan, a strategy in mind, to be executed just as He had pre-determined. How do we know? He told us ahead of time through His prophets. Now, it was only revealed "here a little and there a little" (Isaiah 28:10), but when we come to the New Testament it all makes perfect sense. God is telling us what He had in mind from the beginning.

THE CHURCH IN THE MYSTERY OF THE AGES

Can we not say the same, therefore, concerning the kingdom of Christ? The Old Testament reveals that through Christ "all the nations of the earth would be blessed" (Genesis 12:3); and that He would be a light to the Gentiles (Isaiah 49:6).

Paul explains that the fulfillment of these promises is in the church. Read carefully Ephesians 3:1-11:

128

"For this reason I, Paul, the prisoner of Jesus Christ for you Gentiles if indeed you have heard of the dispensation of the grace of God which was given to me for you, how that by revelation He made known to me the mystery (as I wrote before in a few words, by which, when you read, you may understand my knowledge in the mystery of Christ), which in other ages was not made known to the sons of men, as it has now been revealed by the Spirit to His holy apostles and prophets: that the Gentiles should be fellow heirs, of the same body, and partakers of His promise in Christ through the gospel, of which I became a minister according to the gift of the grace of God given to me by the effective working of His power. To me, who am less than the least of all the saints, this grace was given, that I should preach among the Gentiles the unsearchable riches of Christ, and to make all people see what is the fellowship of the mystery, which from the beginning of the ages has been hidden in God who created all things through Jesus Christ; to the intent that now the manifold wisdom of God might be made known by the church to the principalities and powers in the heavenly places, according to the eternal purpose which He accomplished in Christ Jesus our Lord."

The fact that the church now exists is solely because of the manifold wisdom and eternal purpose of God. The fact that Jews and Gentiles alike can, through the gospel, share in the fellowship of Christ is according to the manifold wisdom and eternal purpose of God. It was God's eternal purpose that the gospel should be preached to every creature (Mark 16:15).

God determined from the foundation of the world that the gospel would be preached to Jews and Gentiles alike, thus creating one new nation, a royal priesthood, a spiritual house built upon the one and only foundation of Jesus Christ, His Son.

According to God's eternal purpose, He spoke of the eternal kingdom. We read of this prophecy in Daniel 2:44 and we read that it has now been received in Hebrews 12:28. The church is that kingdom that shall stand forever.

The Lord's church was not established because His kingdom was rejected by Jews. Rather, the church is the kingdom. God's kingdom upon earth is the church. His kingdom has been established according to His enteral purpose.

It is by the manifold wisdom of God that this kingdom would be given a new name *after* the Gentiles should see His righteousness (Isaiah 62:1-2; 65:15). This would signify an everlasting covenant (Isaiah 61:8), and it would be an everlasting name (Isaiah 56:5).

In Acts chapter ten we read of the first Gentile converts to Christ and, what do you suppose we find next, but a new name being given – "And the disciples were first called Christians in Antioch" (Acts 11:26).

Who was it that gave them this name? According to Isaiah, "The Gentiles shall see your righteousness, and all kings your glory. You shall be called by a new name, which the mouth of the Lord will name" (Isaiah 62:2).

Now, if it is true that the name "Christian" has been given by the manifold wisdom and eternal purpose of God, and that it signifies an everlasting covenant God has made with His people – the church – by what wisdom and purpose do we have authority to call ourselves by any other name? And what covenant is signified by any other name? And, in what other name is there salvation? "Nor is there salvation in any other, for there is no other name under heaven given among men by which we must be saved" (Acts 4:12). There is no other name under heaven given among men whereby we must be saved.

In what other name is there glory? God associates His glory with His name. Note, "I am the Lord, that is My name; and My glory I will not give to another, nor My praise to graven images" (Isaiah 42:8); and again "...how should My name be profaned? And I will not give My glory to another" (Isaiah 48:11). "Therefore God also has highly exalted Him and given Him the name which is above every name, that at the name of Jesus every knee should bow, of those in heaven, and of those on earth, and of those under the earth, and that every tongue should confess that Jesus Christ is Lord, to the glory of God the Father" (Philippians 2:9-11).

We call ourselves Christians, not because some man had an idea of what we should be called, but because of the eternal purpose of God, hidden throughout the ages, but now made known unto men in these last days.

THE NEW COVENANT IN THE MYSTERY OF THE AGES

God gave His Son to taste death for every man (Hebrews 2:9). As a matter of the divine wisdom and revelation of God, God intended to send His Son into this world to crush the head of Satan. He purposed to accomplish this feat, not through many families but one – the family of Abraham.

To keep Abraham's family in check, so that His Son would not be born into an idolatrous nation, God added the law to serve as a schoolmaster, because of their transgressions. From time to time, God revealed portions of His eternal will through prophets and others, so that when it came to fruition we would know the fullness of His will.

God revealed Christ to the children of Israel through Moses saying, "I will raise up for them a Prophet like you from among their brethren, and will put My words in His mouth, and He shall speak to them all that I command Him. And it shall be that whoever will not hear My words, which He speaks in My name, I will require it of him" (Deuteronomy 18:18-19).

Jesus said of Himself, "For I have come down from heaven, not to do My own will, but the will of Him who sent Me" (John 6:38); and, "He who rejects Me, and does not receive My words, has that which judges him the word that I have spoken will judge him in the last day" (John 12:48).

God revealed to Jeremiah that a new covenant would be established in which He would remember our sins no more (Jeremiah 31:31-34). The writer of Hebrews confirms not only once but twice that we now live under this covenant in Christ (Hebrews 8:8 ff. and 10:16 ff.). Moreover, the writer of Hebrews revealed that this covenant was established by the offering of the body of Christ – "once for all."

Through prophetic utterances, God has made known to us that His Son would come with authority, that we should hearken unto His words, and through His covenant we could be reconciled and forgiven completely. It is in the offering, resurrection, covenant, and return of Christ that Satan's head is crushed and the last enemy, death, shall be destroyed.

IN CONCLUSION

Jesus says "come unto Me all you who are weary and heavy laden and I will give you rest." He did not say that simply because He thought it would be a nice thing to say. He said it because He was making known unto us His Father's eternal plan to save man. He is the way, the truth, and the life, and no man can come unto God except he comes through Jesus Christ (John 14:6).

The question before each one now is simply, "Am I willing to come to God through Jesus Christ?" There is no other way. You must hear and believe the gospel; for "faith comes by hearing and hearing by the word of God" (Romans 10:17). If your convictions are not based upon the word of God, you do not have faith. You might have a very strong opinion, but it is not faith.

Having this biblical faith, you must repent of your sins. You must turn from those things which are causing God to turn His face from you. "For the eyes of the Lord are on the righteous, and his ears are open to their prayers; but the face of the Lord is against those who do evil" (1 Peter 3:12).

Having decided to turn from the evil that has severed your relationship with God, it is now time to confess your faith in Christ "unto salvation" (Romans 10:9-10). Someone may say, "Well, I've not confessed Him, but I've never denied Him." That's what Christ said was impossible to do. You might as well as deny Him, if you are going to refuse to confess Him. If you won't confess Him, you'll be denying Him every day of your life.

Another will say, "Oh, I've confessed him. I believe Jesus is God's Son, but I've never obeyed His word to become a Christian." You need to be more consistent than that. Act upon what you believe. Right now, you're no better off than the devils who believe and tremble (James 2:19).

You must be born again. "Except a man is born again, He shall not see the kingdom of heaven... Except a man is born of water and Spirit, he will not enter the kingdom of heaven" (John 3:3, 5).

Upon your confession, you must be baptized into Christ. "For you are all sons of God through faith in Christ Jesus. For as many of you as were baptized into Christ have put on Christ" (Galatians 3:26-27).

When one is baptized scripturally as Paul taught, he comes into a spiritual union with Christ and is brought into harmony with and blessed by the eternal purpose and wisdom of God. He is Christ's and is an heir to the promise made to Abraham.

It is a very special thing to obey the gospel. When you obey the gospel, you are accepting and obeying God's plan created even before the foundation of the world. The religion of Christ is sacred and eternal. It can be your religion, if you will accept and obey your Lord. We invite you now to accept the religion of Christ.

WHY I WANT TO GO TO HEAVEN

Within our Bibles, we read of place that is called heaven. It is the celestial city of God. It is the home prepared by Christ for the redeemed. Heaven awaits the faithful. Heaven is our hope, our goal.

I cannot speak for you, but I want heaven to be my eternal home. I want to go to heaven. I want my family to go to heaven. I want my congregation to go to heaven. I even want my enemies to repent, obey the gospel, and go to heaven. While I cannot speak for you, I am sure that you feel the same way.

In this lesson, I wish to share with you four reasons why I want to go to heaven. Let us "think on these things" and find encouragement and instruction from God's word.

TO AVOID THE HORRORS OF HELL

In the first place, and if for no other reason, I want to go to heaven to avoid the horrors of hell. Certainly this is a sufficient reason! Every one of us will live somewhere forever. There are only two possible destinations for the soul – heaven or hell.

Someday all who are in the graves shall hear the voice of the Son of God and come forth, either to a resurrection of reward or a resurrection of damnation (John 5:28-29). It is a life or death decision. There is a wide gate and broad way that leads to death and many will choose that path; and, there is a strait gate and narrow way that leads to life and relatively few will find it, especially when compared to the vast number that will choose the broad way.

Hell will be a lake of fire (Revelation 20:14) and a place of everlasting punishment for the wicked (Matthew 25:46); where the smoke of their torment will ascend forever and ever (Revelation 14:11); where the worm will never die, and the fire will not be quenched (Mark 9:48). Hell is going to be a place created by God and intentionally forsaken. It is going to be a God-forsaken place of outer darkness filled with the weeping of the wicked and the gnashing teeth of the lost (Matthew 25:30). I don't want to go to that awful place and I don't want you to go there either.

Four categories of being will be in hell. First of all, the devil and his angels will be in hell. In fact, the everlasting fire of hell has been prepared specifically for the devil and his angels (Matthew 25:41). Satan will not be ruling in hell as some artists have depicted. He will not be satisfied in hell. He will be destroyed "in the midst of the stones of fire" (Ezekiel 28:14). Satan and his angels will be suffering and gnashing their teeth in hell just like all of its other residents.

God does not desire for any man to be lost and spend eternity in hell. God longs to see every man repent and be saved (2 Peter 3:9). He sent His only Son to die for the salvation of every man. But, if you choose to live with Satan in this life, God is more than willing to let you live with him in the next life. If you think so much of the devil that you are willing to forsake the love and mercy that caused God to send His only Son to die for you, God will just let you and Satan remain together forever.

A second category of people will be in hell. Hell will also be a place for the fearfully surprised. Jesus is going to tell them, "Depart from Me, you cursed, into the everlasting fire prepared for the devil and his angels" (Matthew 25:41). You will have fearfully surprised Christians crying out, "Lord, when did we see You hungry or thirsty or a stranger or naked or sick or in prison, and did not minister to You?" (Matthew 25:44). Jesus is going to answer them by saying,

"Assuredly, I say to you, inasmuch as you did not do it to one of the least of these, you did not do it to Me" (Matthew 25:45). "And these will go away into everlasting punishment, but the righteous into eternal life" (Matthew 25:46).

Some Christians have lived their lives dictating the terms of their faith to God, rather than obeying His commandments. Sadly, it is going to take the Judgment Day for them to see the foolishness of their attitude toward God and His word. It is not for man to tell God what he will or will not do. God speaks and we obey. "Speak Lord, for thy servant hears!"

You're going to have fearfully surprised souls who lived and died in the wrong religion. Jesus said, "Not everyone who says to Me, 'Lord, Lord,' shall enter the kingdom of heaven, but he who does the will of My Father in heaven. Many will say to Me in that day, 'Lord, Lord, have we not prophesied in Your name, cast out demons in Your name, and done many wonders in Your name?' And then I will declare to them, 'I never knew you; depart from Me, you who practice lawlessness!'" (Matthew 7:21-23).

These souls believe they are saved when, truthfully, they have never even obeyed the gospel. They have been loyal to the doctrines and commandments of men, but not to the gospel of Christ. Jesus said, "I never knew you." Only those who obey Him are known of Him. Paul has said, "...you who are troubled rest with us when the Lord Jesus is revealed from heaven with His mighty angels, in flaming fire taking vengeance on those who do not know God, and on those who do not obey the gospel of our Lord Jesus Christ. These shall be punished with everlasting destruction from the presence of the Lord and from the glory of His power..." (2 Thessalonians 1:7-9).

A third category of people will be in hell. In hell, there will be those who left Christ and never returned. I'm sure we each know of a brother or sister in Christ who has left the Lord and has yet to return. While we are praying for them to come home, we must also admonish them to repent or be lost forever.

The Bible says, "For if, after they have escaped the pollutions of the world through the knowledge of the Lord and Savior Jesus Christ, they are again entangled in them and overcome, the latter end is worse for them than the beginning. For it would have been better for them not to have known the way of righteousness, than having known it, to turn from the holy commandment delivered to them" (2 Peter 2:20-21).

We must do what we can to save them. If necessary, we must "save with fear, pulling them out of the fire, hating even the garment defiled by the flesh" (Jude 23). Only when they are turned from the error of their way will their soul be saved from death (James 5:19).

Lastly, a fourth category of people will be in hell. In hell, there will be those who care not for Christ and have no regard for their own soul. However, just because a person may not have a high regard for his soul or for eternity does not in any way negate the fact that he has a soul and will in fact live somewhere forever. Ignoring the facts will not make them go away. Living like there is no God, does not change the fact that He is alive and well.

The Bible clearly states that hell is a place of punishment for "the cowardly, unbelieving, abominable, murderers, sexually immoral, sorcerers, idolaters, and all liars" (Revelation 21:8). I do not want to live that way. I do not want to face that destiny. I don't want to have that kind of person as my neighbor now. Why would I want to have them as my neighbors for eternity?

Just the other day, it was a cool autumn day of maybe sixty-five degrees, I was doing some yard work and I'll have to say I became quite parched. I went to my truck and found a bottle of water which had just barely a decent drop left in it. I'll have to say that was the best drop of water that I had in sometime.

Now, this experience got me thinking about hell. You know, there will be no drops of water in hell. If a person can be thirsty for a drop of water on a sixty-five degree autumn day, how much more do you think he'll beg for that drop of water in hell?

As I was thinking, I came to the conclusion that if we could spend only one minute in hell, it should be enough for us to give the rest of our days in humble service to God. Now I know this is impossible; but if you will just imagine for a moment that intense heat, the awful cries, the hopeless expressions on the faces you will see, I believe every lost soul would be begging for relief after only one minute – one minute in hell.

If you really believed how terrible and how real this place is, you would want to stay out of there. I believe there will be untold cries of an infinite number begging for one more chance to repent – just one! They are not going to need to hear sermon after sermon! They would only need the chance to obey the gospel – just the chance.

I can hear their cries now: "We'll come to you, Lord!" "We'll obey your word!" "We'll be happy to serve you!" "We'll do whatever you want, Lord!" However, those prayers will never be heard.

The Lord has cast them out and forever blocked them from His mind. A man in hell doesn't think about honoring his parents or his wife above God. He doesn't think about going fishing instead of going to church. He doesn't believe one church is as good as another. He doesn't believe all he has to be is a good person.

After one minute in hell, that man realizes how foolish those beliefs are and all he wants is one chance to repent. But, all he can think about is the lifetime he had to repent!

Some people are foolish enough to believe that if they worship Satan in this life, he will take care of them and honor them in hell. After just one minute, those people will realize there is no honor in hell.

The Bible teaches us that Satan will be cast down and made to suffer just like everyone else. God has promised to destroy him. After all, hell is a place prepared specifically for him (Matthew 25:41).

He'll be begging for a drop of water just like everyone else. You may think you can beg him for water. But, he'll be the first to tell you to learn to like it! There'll be no help in hell! Oh, how I want to stay out of that awful place! I want to go to heaven if for no other reason than to stay out of that awful place.

TO EXPERIENCE THE JOYS OF HEAVEN

Secondly, I want to live a faithful, godly, Christian life so that I can experience the joys of heaven. I want to go to heaven so that I can experience the joy of that blessed home of the soul. I want to be there with my Savior. I want to kiss Him and worship at His feet. I want to live in that land that knows no parting, and where tears shall never dim the eye (Revelation 21:4). We will not have to worry about pain or death any more. Our days will be filled with bliss and our souls with eternal gladness. The pure water of the river of life shall flow as clearly as crystal (Revelation 22:1) and

140

light shall radiate from the very presence of God. The voices of all the redeemed shall blend in one accord to the Lamb that was slain and the Father whose face we shall at last see as He sits upon His glory-circled throne. How beautiful heaven must be!

I want to go to heaven. I want to see the mansion my Savior has prepared for me. I want to meet my heavenly neighbors. I want to bask in the light of God's redeeming love while the ceaseless ages forever roll.

Likewise, I believe if we could spend only one minute in heaven, we would never want to leave. I know how hard it is to say goodbye to a faithful child of God. But, I also believe they would not trade places with us for anything.

"How beautiful heaven must be!
Sweet home of the happy and free!
Fair haven of rest for the weary,
How beautiful heaven must be!"

Imagine just one minute in heaven, and you'll see why the Christian life is worth more than anything. Just one minute in heaven, when faith shall become sight, will prove to us the wisdom of our decision to obey the gospel. Just one minute in heaven, and we'll see how right the Bible truly is and how wise it was to obey God rather than men. Just one minute in heaven, and we'll be forever glad that we decided to worship and serve God in spirit and truth – that we did not take our religion into our own hands. Just one minute in heaven, and we'll know how right it was to follow Christ and heed His commandments. After just one minute in heaven, we'll be thanking the Holy Spirit for the truth He revealed (John16:13). Oh, how want to go to heaven and share its glory with you!

In heaven, with the Godhead and the holy angels, will also be those who died in obedience to the Lord under vari-

141

ous covenants before the cross. Those like Abraham and Job who died as Patriarchs will be there. Others like Moses and Daniel, who died faithfully under the Old Law will be there.

You will get to meet great heroes of the Old Testament. You will also be reunited with faithful Christians. All who have died in the Lord will be there (Revelation 14:13). And, in addition to these faithful people who populate heaven will be the innocents who died without being marred by sin. They died being "alive apart from the law" (Romans 7:9).

Consider now these three groups of people. If you are of the age of reasonable mental accountability, you cannot go to heaven as one who is in a safe condition. You have sinned and your sins need to be atoned. Neither can you go to heaven as a patriarch or under the Law of Moses, for those dispensations have ended. The only way you can go to heaven is by obeying the gospel and living a faithful Christian life. The blood of Christ must grant atonement for your sins.

TO BE GATHERED UNTO MY PEOPLE

A third reason for my desire to go to heaven is to be gathered unto my people. "Thus link by link the strong is chain broken that binds us to earth, and our passage soothed to another world."

I want to see my family again. I want to know that I will again see my grandmother who helped teach and strengthen me in the gospel. I will want to see my children again. I will want to see my wife again. "O' that we might be at last united in that heaven of rest, where trouble and sorrow never enter, to join in an everlasting chorus of praise and glory to our Lord and Savior!"

142

In this life we have to say goodbye and let go of the people we love most. Upon losing his son, King David said, "I shall go to him, but he shall not return to me" (2 Samuel 12:23). To let go of those we love is a very hard thing for us to do. But, in heaven, we will never have to let go of them again.

I think of the loving wife who nurtured her sickly husband throughout his remaining days. I think of parents who had to say goodbye to their children much too soon. I think of brothers and sisters devastated by death's cold hand, and I am thankful that these are experiences for this life *only*.

I'd like to be there to see that husband a wife reunited. I'd like to witness those parents seeing their child again. I believe this will only add to the great joy of that "Summerland of Bliss."

I also want to be with those who I have seen obey the Lord, "that I may rejoice in the day of Christ, that I have not run in vain, neither labored in vain" (Philippians 2:16). I want to know that they made it safely; that they finished their course and kept the faith. I'd like to know that my willingness to work for the Lord paid eternal dividends for some dear soul. I'd like to see these people again, because many of them have become some of my dearest friends on earth.

I also consider "my people" to be the faithful men and women who will have gone on before me. "Blessed are the dead which die in the Lord from henceforth: Yea, saith the Spirit, that they may rest from their labors: and their works do follow them" (Revelation 14:13, KJV).

I want to see Abraham, Isaac, and Jacob. I want to meet Peter, James, and John. I'd like to embrace Paul and shake his hand. I also want to see all those faithful gospel preachers of yesteryear that I never had a chance to meet in this life. I want to see all the loving, faithful preachers, elders, teachers, and members of the Lord's church who encouraged me to preach the word and took me under their wing to teach me the way of the Lord more perfectly. Truly, "the memory of the righteous is blessed" (Proverbs 10:7).

TO HEAR "WELL DONE"

Lastly, I want to go to heaven so that I may hear "Well done good and faithful servant." I want to know and hear that Jesus was well-pleased with my miniscule efforts. I have not done enough. I can never do enough to measure up to His deserving worth. I have failed Him many times in many ways. But, I know that I can repent of those failures and be faithful with the abilities and opportunities He grants me.

I had a great-uncle who had a keen way of stating things. He once said, "Everyone loves a compliment." I believe this is true. As a boy and later as a man, if my father complimented my efforts, I would double-down and work even harder. I was happy to know he was pleased. Even more so, I am happy to think of that day when the Savior will express His pleasure at our service. Beloved, if we will finish our course, someday the Lord – the righteous Judge – will say to us, "Come, ye blessed of my Father, inherit the kingdom prepared for you from the foundation of the world" (Matthew 25:34). If we will keep the faith, the Lord will give to each of us a crown of righteousness just as He gave Paul, and to all those who have loved Him (2 Timothy 4:8).

IN CONCLUSION

I want to go to heaven and I want you to come with me. For any man to enter heaven he must be born again (John 3:3-5). He must obey the Lord (Hebrews 5:9). Christ beckons now, "Come unto Me…" He is awaiting your decision, "Behold, I stand at the door and knock…" Heaven's gates are swung wide open for you, "The Spirit and the Bride say come…" Come and go with us!

THE JUDGMENT DAY

I would like to discuss with you one of the most serious matters you or I will ever discuss. I'd like to talk with you about the Judgment Day – that divine appointment we all must keep. Let us begin our study with a reading of Revelation 20:11-15: "Then I saw a great white throne and Him who sat on it, from whose face the earth and the heaven fled away. And there was found no place for them. And I saw the dead, small and great, standing before God, and books were opened. And another book was opened, which is the Book of Life. And the dead were judged according to their works, by the things which were written in the books. The sea gave up the dead who were in it, and Death and Hades delivered up the dead who were in them. And they were judged, each one according to his works. Then Death and Hades were cast into the lake of fire. This is the second death. And anyone not found written in the Book of Life was cast into the lake of fire."

You will observe that the greatest crowd ever is assembled. The greatest Judge ever is presiding. The greatest books are opened. And, the greatest sentence is rendered. Everyone will be assembled on that day of final judgment. You will be there and I will be there. Kings and peasants alike shall stand before the Son of God. Your favorite movie star, musician, and athlete will be there. Every man who has ever lived will have his record read to him from the Book Life. Every one of us will have to give an account for that which we have done, whether it is good or evil (2 Corinthians 5:10).

On that day, you may look to your left or right and see such notable figures as George Washington, Thomas Jefferson, or Abraham Lincoln. Regardless of who you may see, you will be just as important as anyone there. As far as your soul is concerned, you will be the most important person there.

The Judgment Day is going to be a great day of reckoning for each of us. On that day, every knee shall bow and every tongue shall confess (Romans 14:11). It will be a day in which all who have ever lived will receive justice. The Lord says, "And behold, I am coming quickly, and My reward is with Me, to give to every one according to his work" (Revelation 22:12).

On that day, the Lord, the righteous Judge, is going to set the record straight. Just the thought of it ought to make us tremble. Yet, I can tell by the way people are living now, that many souls simply do not appreciate the greatness of the Judgment Day. Many are failing to prepare. Some may even think that everyone will be saved in the end. That simply is not true. Jesus has taught us that many will be lost compared to the relatively few that will be saved. Jesus admonishes us to, "Enter by the narrow gate; for wide is the gate and broad is the way that leads to destruction, and there are many who go in by it. Because narrow is the gate and difficult is the way which leads to life, and there are few who find it" (Matthew 7:13-14).

I suppose some people may believe they will be able to cry for mercy at the Judgment. Friends, it will be too late for mercy then. The time for mercy and pardon is now. The Day of Judgment will be a day of justice and retribution. "For we know Him who said, 'Vengeance is Mine; I will repay, says the Lord.' And again, 'The Lord will judge His people'" (Hebrews 10:30).

Knowing of the seriousness and certainty of the final judgment, Paul wrote, "Knowing, therefore, the terror of the Lord, we persuade men..." (2 Corinthians 5:11).

NO POSTPONEMENT

Allow me to share a few thoughts with you about the Judgement Day which may help us to take it more seriously. In the first place, there will be no postponement of the Judgment Day.

I am aware that sometimes those charged with an offense will postpone judgment and ask for a continuance. God will not be granting any continuance at the final judgment. God has already "appointed a day in which He will judge the world in righteousness by that man whom He has ordained and given assurance unto all men in that He has raised Him from the dead" (Acts 17:31).

God knows the day and the hour His Son will return (Matthew 24:36). On that day, and in that hour, this world and all that is therein will be burned up (2 Peter 3:10-13). All of this will happen in the "twinkling of an eye" (1 Corinthians 15:52). A person would not have time to ask God to postpone the judgment even if he wanted.

NO ESCAPE

In the second place, we will not be able to escape God's judgment. Sometimes the guilty will escape judgment by changing their names, addresses, and even their appearances. They may move halfway around the world, and stay on the move, so that they can escape punishment for their crimes. This will not be the case on the day of God's reckoning. One cannot escape the Judgment Day. Every guilty soul is going to come face to face with Jesus and look Him in the eyes and explain to Him why He died in vain for them. Those who refused and rejected Christ, those who mocked Him and blasphemed His holy name, even those Christians who turned their backs to Him will come face to face with Jesus. And friends, there will be no escape. Every one of us will have to give an account of our deeds to God.

NO HIDING THE EVIDENCE

Thirdly, no one will be able to hide the evidence that has mounting against them. "And be sure your sin will find you out." Many times, criminals walk freely because they were successful at hiding or destroying any and all incriminating evidence that would have placed them behind bars. However, on the Judgment Day all the evidence will be brought to light. "For God will bring every work into judgment, including every secret thing, whether it is good or whether it is evil" (Ecclesiastes 12:14).

Men cannot hide themselves from God. "And there is no creature hidden from His sight, but all things are naked and open to the eyes of Him to whom we must give account" (Hebrews 4:13). Sometimes we try to hide the evidence of our sins from others and even from ourselves. Sometimes we are successful. But, you cannot succeed in hiding your sins from God. "For if our heart condemns us, God is greater than our heart, and knows all things" (1 John 3:20).

"Woe to those who seek deep to hide their counsel far from the Lord, and their works are in the dark; they say, 'Who sees us?' and, 'Who knows us?'" (Isaiah 29:15). Ah, friend, God is there! God sees and God knows; and God will bring every secret thing to judgment.

NO BUYING VERDICTS

On the Judgment Day, there will be no buying verdicts. Many times criminals can successfully bribe corrupt jurors or juries to escape justice. However, on that day, all the money in the world will not save you when your sins have damned your soul. The Lord cannot be corrupted. He is the righteous Judge and His judgements are true and righteous.

Let also make another connection with the righteous judgments of God; namely, there will be no unfair bias on the Judgment Day. On some occasions, a criminal has been set free simply because of *whom* they were or who they *knew*. I think we can each relate to some past experience of unrighteous prejudice in our courts. However, on the Judgment Day, every one of us shall be judged impartially. In Colossians 3:24-25, Paul makes a point that those who serve the Lord will receive their inheritance from the Lord, but "he who does wrong will be repaid for the wrong which he has done, and there is no partiality."

Peter had the right understanding of this concept when he said, "In truth I perceive that God shows no partiality. But in every nation whoever fears Him and works righteousness is accepted by Him" (Acts 10:34-35).

NO MISTRIAL

Neither will you see a mistrial or overturned verdict on the Judgment Day. Sometimes you will read of a mistrial being granted because something was not done properly in the first trial. However, "The judgments of the Lord are true and righteous altogether" (Psalms 19:9). You will see no mistrials resulting from the Judgment Day.

If you are found guilty it will be because you were guilty in the eyes of God. If you are found blameless, it will be because the blood of Christ washed you clean and you were, therefore, found blameless in the eyes of God. Either way, you will not be mistaken for someone else or condemned of something you did not do.

NO PLEA BARGAIN

A person will not be able to "plea bargain" to keep from appearing before the Judge. Job understood that God is not like man, "that I may answer Him, and that we should go to court together" (Job 9:32). We cannot bargain with God. Either we choose to obey Him or we choose to disobey Him. We either choose to walk in light or darkness, but there is no bargaining.

Also, the point of the plea bargain is to avoid court and to accept a lesser punishment than the one deserving. Friends, do not look for this on the Judgment Day. The punishment which will be handed out will be the same for all – "everlasting destruction from the presence of the Lord and the glory of His power" (2 Thessalonians 1:9)

NO HIGHER COURT OF APPEALS

Oftentimes, we will hear of an appeal being made to a higher court, maybe even all the way to the Supreme Court. Yet, on the Judgment Day, every one of us shall be judged by the Highest Court ever known; and the decision will be eternal – eternal life or death (Matthew 25:46).

The verdict rendered at the final judgment will never be appealed or overturned. It will be a judgment you will have to live with for all eternity.

IN CONCLUSION

Do you have boldness in the Day of Judgment (1 John 4:17)? Would you like to have boldness in the Day of Judgment? If the Lord was to come today, or the cold hand of death was to take you right now, would you be ready just like you are? If the doctor told you, "This is all I can do for you. This is it." – What would occupy your mind? A dying man cannot help but to think of his relationship with God.

But, I tell you, we are all *dying men*! We can't stop it. It's going to happen eventually. "It is appointed for man once to die and then the judgment" (Hebrews 9:27).

Just imagine with me that this is the Judgment Day and we are now standing before the bar on high. We are now looking into the eyes of Jesus Christ. His voice seizes our attention.

Some He commends by saying: "Come, you blessed of My Father." Others, however, He sentences to outer darkness where there will be weeping and gnashing of teeth.

When He turns His attention to you, calls your name, and reads your record, what will He say? It is not a question of *if* we shall stand before Him, but *how* shall we stand before Him? Will I stand before my Lord as a faithful, obedient Christian – a child of God? Or, will I stand before Him as some profane person, like Esau, who sold my soul for the passing pleasures of this life?

ALL-SUFFICIENT RELIGION

The Christian religion is an all-sufficient religion. When we live and teach according to the perfect law of liberty, and conduct ourselves as God would have us, our religion is the most beautiful thing on earth! It is perfect, complete, entire, and in need of nothing further to accomplish God's intended purpose. When we choose not to live and teach according to the gospel of Christ, we have an insufficient religion – a vain religion. I presume no one wants to be guilty of having a vain religion. I suppose with confidence that each one of us desires a religion that is pure and undefiled – well-pleasing to God.

In order to have such a religion, one must be able to distinguish between vain religion and pure religion. In order to have the correct religion, one must have the correct standard of religion whereby to make an appeal. The Christian faith, as God would have it, is revealed finally and fully in the New Testament "once and for all" (Jude 3). He has given unto us "all things that pertain to life and godliness, through the knowledge of Him who called us by glory and virtue" (2 Peter 1:3).

When we base our beliefs solely upon the all-sufficient plan of God, we can believe as Paul believed, "Not that we are sufficient of ourselves to think of anything as being from ourselves, but our sufficiency is from God" (2 Corinthians 3:5). When we trust in God almighty for the plan and purpose of our religion, we can truthfully say, "Our sufficiency is from God."

Man must not be found working backwards by forming an opinion *first* and *then* consulting to the Bible to see *if* God agrees. Oftentimes, this is exactly what is done. A person determines what he believes to be true, and then merely consults the Bible. When a person takes this approach, he will find anything remotely resembling his preconceived convictions and the Scriptures will be twisted (2 Peter 3:16). It seems to me that this is one of the ways a man can oppose himself (2 Timothy 2:25). Such an approach to the Scriptures leads to false doctrine and contradiction. Such an approach will surely lead one astray (2 Peter 3:17).

We must start with the Scriptures and then make a decision as to whether or not we understand and will obey what God has said. "Faith comes by hearing and hearing by the word of God" (Romans 10:17). We must study the Bible first and then apply what God has said. Anything otherwise, is merely an attempt to take our religion into our own hands, and determine the rightness of our religion without God.

Dear friends, God has given us a perfect religion, if we will only accept it. In this lesson, I want to study with you three aspects of the Christian religion in order to help you understand the rightness of His cause.

THE ALL-SUFFICIENT CHRIST

In this first place, Christianity is all-sufficient because of the all-sufficient Christ. It is amazing to consider the absolute perfection and finality of the offering of Christ. The writer of Hebrews teaches us of God's will in offering Christ and that, "By that will we have been sanctified through the offering of the body of Jesus Christ once for all" (Hebrews 10:10). Furthermore, "...this Man, after He had offered one sacrifice for sins forever, sat down at the right hand of God" (Hebrews 10:12). His offering was "once for all" and "one sacrifice for sins forever." This world will never need another Savior. We will never need another sacrifice for our sins.

The blood of Jesus is perfect and complete. His offering was all-sufficient to cleanse us from our sins. Just think how many sins you commit in a day. Just consider how many sins you've committed in your life. Think about how many sins are committed by the people of this world in a day. It has to be an enormously staggering figure! And just think, if this world stands for a trillion years from now, how many sins we will commit. Yet, the blood of Jesus is so perfect, so complete, that this one single, monumental sacrifice is entirely sufficient for God to forgive every last sin, if man will only accept it.

If we will only trust in God and accept the way He provides for us, we can all be saved. Jesus Christ tasted death for every man (Hebrews 2:9). He is the propitiation – the means of atoning – for the whole world (1 John 2:2). You will never need another Savior. Beloved, you will never *have* another Savior!

The all-sufficient Christ also serves His brethren as the all-sufficient mediator and advocate between us and God. Paul wrote Timothy, "For there is one God and one Mediator between God and men, the Man Christ Jesus, who gave Himself a ransom for all, to be testified in due time" (1 Timothy 2:5-6). In light of this passage, it is absurd to believe that Mary, any departed saint, or so-called priest, pastor, or prophet was ever intended to serve in this capacity. Paul said there is *one* mediator and that mediator is Christ.

The apostle John wrote, "My little children, these things I write to you, that you may not sin. And if anyone sins, we have an Advocate with the Father, Jesus Christ the righteous" (1 John 2:1). John said that our Advocate is Jesus Christ the righteous, not Mary, Muhammad, Joseph Smith or anyone else.

Christians are complete in Christ. "For in Him dwells all the fullness of the Godhead bodily; and you are complete in Him, who is the head of all principality and power" (Colossians 2:9-10). By His resurrection, God has made Jesus our Lord and Christ (Acts 2:36). He has all power or authority in heaven and in earth and we are to obey Him (Matthew 28:18, 20). Jesus Christ "is the blessed and only Potentate, the King of kings and Lord of lords" (1 Timothy 6:15).

THE ALL-SUFFICIENT CREED

The careful Bible student will also observe that the Christian religion is all-sufficient because of its all-sufficient creed. The word of God "is given by inspiration of God, and is profitable for doctrine, for reproof, for correction, for instruction in righteousness, that the man of God may be complete, thoroughly equipped for every good work" (2 Timothy 3:16-17).

God's word will accomplish its intended purpose. "For as the rain comes down, and the snow from heaven, and do not return there, but water the earth, and make it bring forth and bud, that it may give seed to the sower and bread to the eater, So shall My word be that goes forth from My mouth; it shall not return to Me void, but it shall accomplish what I please, and it shall prosper in the thing for which I sent it" (Isaiah 55:10-11).

Man has no need for any manmade creed book when he has the Bible. God's word is truth (John 17:17). The word of God is not *some* truth, but "all truth" (John 16:13). It is perfect. It is able to set you free (John 8:31-32). Obedience to the word of God will purify your souls (1 Peter 1:22). We are sanctified and cleansed "with the washing of water by the word" (Ephesians 5:26).

158

I was once visited by two very young Mormon "elders." I asked them if they believed the Bible. They said they did. I asked them if they believed it was the inspired word of God. They said they did. I then asked them if they believed Jesus when He said the Holy Spirit would guide the apostles into "all truth" (John 16:13). They said, "Yes." I then proceeded to ask them, "Where in 'all truth' as it was revealed to the apostles by the Holy Spirit do we read of Joseph Smith, the Book of Mormon, or the Church of Latter-Day Saints?"

Is this not what we should be asking anyone belonging to a church or engaged in any religious practice which cannot be found in the Bible? Why spend a day in any church not revealed in God's word? God's word must be our authority. It does not have some authority, but all authority. The gospel is God's power or authority to save man from his sins (Romans 1:16-17). And, even if an angel from heaven preaches another gospel, we cannot accept it as truth (Galatians 1:6-10).

The word of God is the all-sufficient word of truth by which men are sanctified and born again. We cannot add to or take from that which God has deemed complete. When we come to understand and appreciate the all-sufficient authority of the word of God, we will be able to do as Paul instructed Titus and "speak with all authority" (Titus 2:15). We know that our authority does not come from us, but from the word of God. Our purpose is not to supplant or replace God's word, but simply to teach it in sincerity and truth.

No man, council, congregation, or creed has ever had the authority to usurp, supplement or substitute the authority Christ has over His church —in any way — though many have tried. The church must be found submissive to the authority of Christ in all things (see Ephesians 1:22 and Colos-

159

sians 1:18). Christ has all authority in His church, and by His authority we have our creed – the Bible.

The Holy Spirit guided the apostles into all truth. The gospel He has given is profitable for doctrine and every good work. And not even an angel from heaven has the authority to add to it. Thus, we must never think more of men than the word which is written (1 Corinthians 4:6).

Only when we return to the Bible and the Bible alone as our sole rule for faith and practice will we speak the same thing, mind the same thing, and there will be no division among us (1 Corinthians 1:10-13; Philippians 3:16-18).

The seed of the kingdom is the word of God (Luke 8:11). Only when the seed is planted in the heart and obeyed will a Christian be produced. While it is true that early Christians wrote creeds to distinguish themselves from heresies and the reformers believed they were acting righteously in producing creeds to distinguish themselves from Catholicism, such actions were quite clearly superfluous, as the only document needed to distinguish one from the other is the New Testament of Jesus Christ. The result of such creeds has been more division, greater confusion, and a multiplicity of churches never found in the Bible.

THE ALL-SUFFICIENT CHURCH

Lastly, the all-sufficiency of the Christian faith can be appreciated by understanding the all-sufficient church. Paul's letter to the Ephesians is perhaps the greatest source for understanding this spiritual truth. Herein, Paul teaches that the church is the spiritual body of Christ.

Note, "And He (God) put all things under His (Christ) feet, and gave Him to be head over all things to the church, which is His body, the fullness of Him who fills all in all" (Ephesians 1:22-23). According to Paul the church is the body of Christ, the fullness of Christ, and there is only "one body" (Ephesians 4:4).

Men of every nation, people, kindred, and tongue are called out of the darkness of sin by the gospel of Christ (2 Thessalonians 2:14) and assembled in Christ by almighty God (Acts 2:47) to form the spiritual body of Christ – the church of Christ (Romans 16:16).

The church of Christ is the kingdom of Christ. The term kingdom denotes the form of government ruling the church. We are called out of the kingdom of darkness and added to the kingdom of God's dear Son (Colossians 1:13).

Of course the kingdom, or church, now exists, for otherwise we could not be added thereto. "Therefore, since we are receiving a kingdom which cannot be shaken, let us have grace, by which we may serve God acceptably with reverence and godly fear" (Hebrews 12:28).

In the church, we have all grace whereby to enter and to serve. All spiritual blessings are in Christ (Ephesians 1:3). God has granted "all grace" unto us so that we might have "all sufficiency in all things, (and) have an abundance for every good work" (2 Corinthians 9:8). God promises His people that He will make a way for them to accomplish the work He has purposed for them to do. No other religion on earth has this promise. If you want the promise of all spiritual blessings and all grace abounding toward you, you must be in Christ. You must come to accept the perfect religion of the Son of God.

Such subjects as the organization, worship, and work of the church are surface issues. The enormous issue which lurks beneath the surface is one of respect for the authority of the Bible. Either we have to obey God, or we do not have to obey God. Why do people believe they can replace the biblical organization of the Lord's church with a manmade organization? In short, they do not believe the Bible has to be obeyed on this subject.

Denominationalists have been indoctrinated to believe that they do not have to obey God. These souls have been led to believe that as long as they are sincere and feel satisfied with what they are doing that God will accept them, their agenda, and their decisions. However, when we study the Bible from the Garden of Eden to the celestial Eden of Revelation, we find that those who are accepted of God are those who obey Him. Those who keep His commandments have right to the tree of life and may enter the gates into the city (Revelation 22:14). All others will be left outside of the city (Revelation 21:27; 22:15).

Some dear souls question the all-sufficiency of the Lord's church. Possibly they suppose any institution or any church can do the work or stand in place of the Lord's church. But, look at it in these terms: would you believe another "savior" could do for you what *the* Savior has done? Or, would you believe just any book on religion could stand in the place of *His* Book on religion? Why then would you suppose one church or religious institution could stand in the place of *His* church? We are simply suggesting that you view the all-sufficiency of the Lord's church with the same respect which you hold for the all-sufficiency of His blood, and His word. If every man would do this, every man could be united in this perfect and all-sufficient religion of Christ.

IN CONCLUSION

An all-sufficient religion is based solely upon God's all-sufficient plan and is in need of nothing further. Man must surrender to the all-sufficient Christ by obeying the all-sufficient creed to be added to the all-sufficient church.

If you've never come to Christ in penitent faith to confess His name and be baptized for the forgiveness of sins (as there is no other reason stated in the Scriptures), you ought to do that now. You're going to have to do it. Why not do it now? An all-sufficient religion is the only kind of religion that will please God. The pure, all-sufficient religion of Christ, as it is found in the New Testament, can be yours and is offered to you now by heaven's invitation.

MARRIAGE, DIVORCE, AND REMARRIAGE

For our present study, I wish to call your attention to the matter of marriage, divorce, and remarriage. Our study is not a pleasant one, but an essential one none the less. It is one of great controversy, but this has not always been the case. Once, a time existed in our nation when divorce was seldom known and hardly a preacher anywhere dared to question the word of God on the subject. Times have changed. People today have a propensity for divorce. And, with the rising number of divorces occurring in our families, among our loved ones, and in our churches, some of our preachers, elders, and churches have changed their feelings on this matter.

Times may have changed, but the Bible has not. "Jesus Christ is the same yesterday, today, and forever" (Hebrews 13:8). God has said, "I am the Lord, I do not change..." (Malachi 3:6). The same can be said for His word which "lives and abides forever" (1Peter 1:23). The same can be said for those who faithfully keep His word as "he who does the will of God abides forever" (1 John 2:17). The word of God will read exactly the same on the day of final judgment as it does right now. Jesus teaches us, "He who rejects Me, and does not receive My words, has that which judges him, the word that I have spoken will judge him in the last day" (John 12:48).

It is not for us to change the word of God, but for the word of God to change us. Regardless of how many preachers or elders may argue with or question the word of God on this matter, we are not going to be judged by them or their words. We are going to be judged by the Lord and His word. His say on the matter should be our greatest concern.

His word on the matter is *the* final authority whether we agree with it or not.

MARRIAGE

In the very beginning of time, the sacredness and blessedness of marriage was understood. God viewed His wonderful creation and was pleased with everything He made, with one exception. He said, "It is not good that man should be alone." God desired then, as He desires today, for man to marry and have companionship with woman. Adam, the first husband, understood that the woman created from his rib was "flesh of his flesh and bone of his bones." He said, "Therefore a man shall leave his father and mother and be joined to his wife, and they shall become one flesh" (Genesis 2:24).

From the very beginning, we find stated that marriage is between a man and a woman. It's sad that we have to pause for a moment in our lesson and point out something as clear as that, but these are the times in which we live.

A biblical marriage is a natural union between a man and a woman. Anything otherwise is unnatural (Romans 1:26-27). Marriage is a union of man and woman, husband and wife, which involves both parties leaving father and mother and becoming one flesh, a new family. Jesus adds, "So then, they are no longer two but one flesh. Therefore what God has joined together, let not man separate" (Matthew 19:6).

Marriage is a covenant made between the husband and the wife and is to be honored for life. "For the woman who has a husband is bound by the law to her husband as long as he lives. But if the husband dies, she is released from the law of her husband" (Romans 7:2).

"A wife is bound by law as long as her husband lives; but if her husband dies, she is at liberty to be married to whom she wishes, only in the Lord" (1 Corinthians 7:39).

Marriage is a union that should be "until death do us part." The Scriptures establish the fact that marriage is between a man and woman, who become one flesh, and are not to be separated by any man. The Scriptures teach us that death is the only possible means of a separation between a husband and wife which would not involve sin being committed by someone involved.

The Bible teaches us that wives are to submit themselves to their own husbands, as unto the Lord (Ephesians 5:21). Likewise, husbands are to love their wives as Christ loves the church and gave Himself for it (Ephesians 5:25).

How many more marriages do you think we would see honored "till death do us part" if both parties involved would simply honor the Golden Rule and treat each other as they would like to be treated? If we would just do that, and live that way, we could end this lesson right now and go no further. We would have no need to talk about divorce or remarriage. But, it is because we do not treat one another the way we should that we must proceed to our second point, the subject of divorce.

DIVORCE

It has been said that murder destroys lives, while divorce destroys families. I believe this is true. God hates divorce. Read with me from Malachi 2:15-16: "...Therefore take heed to your spirit, and let none deal treacherously with the wife of his youth. For the Lord God of Israel says that He hates divorce, for it covers one's garment with violence," says the Lord of hosts. "Therefore take heed to your spirit, that you do not deal treacherously."

167

Sometimes I meet people who believe they can divorce, so long as they do not remarry. But, God *hates* divorce. A marriage must not be torn asunder. We should work to save our marriages at all costs. As spouses, we should be more forgiving. We should be more encouraging. We should be more giving and more understanding. We should be more patient and longsuffering. We should seek to live in such a way that it is a great joy and pleasure for our spouse to be "one flesh" with us. We should establish our homes on the principle of the Golden Rule.

However, sometimes a spouse can be downright sinful and violate the marriage bed through their fornication and promiscuity. For this cause, the Lord granted one exception for divorce. "Whoever divorces his wife, except for sexual immorality ("fornication," KJV), and marries another, commits adultery; and whoever marries her who is divorced commits adultery" (Matthew 19:9). Christ gives us one exception that would cause God to accept and grant a divorce, which is "porneia" or "illicit sexual intercourse."

The Pharisees came asking Christ, "Is it lawful for a man to divorce his wife for just any reason?" (Matthew 19:3). They did so "tempting Him." Upon His answer, they continued, "Why then did Moses command to give a certificate of divorce, and to put her away?" Jesus answered, "Moses, because of the hardness of your hearts, permitted you to divorce your wives, but from the beginning it was not so. And I say to you, whoever divorces his wife, except for fornication ("Sexual immorality" is not a good translation. "Porneia" literally means "illicit sexual intercourse."), and marries another, commits adultery; and whoever marries her who is divorced commits adultery" (Matthew 19:8-9).

The Law of Moses permitted divorce, but this was not God's plan from the beginning. The Law of Christ takes us

168

back to the original purpose of the union and states only one reason for divorce – fornication. Also note that fornication is the sexual act. Adultery is the unscriptural union that takes place after an unscriptural divorce. And from Solomon we read, "Whoever commits adultery with a woman lacks understanding; he who does so destroys his own soul" (Proverbs 6:32).

The disciples responded to Christ's teaching by stating, "If such is the case of the man with his wife, it is better not to marry." Now, consider the Lord's reply. He did not back down from what He said. Rather, He put things in the proper perspective. He said:

"All cannot accept this saying, but only those to whom it has been given: For there are eunuchs who were born thus from their mother's womb [*someone incapable of sexual activity from birth*], and there are eunuchs who were made eunuchs by men [*castration was a practice among some*], and there are eunuchs who have made themselves eunuchs for the kingdom of heaven's sake. He who is able to accept it, let him accept it."

A eunuch for the "kingdom of heaven's sake" would be one who has abstained from a marriage relationship in order to please God. You find an example of this when the children of Israel returned from Babylonian captivity, only to begin intermarrying (*again*) with the various heathen people of the area (Ezra 9:1-2). You would think that they would have learned that lesson by now! But here again, they entered into God-forbidden marriages, mingling Israel's seed with others, while taking up the abominable practices as before.

Ezra described this act as a "transgression" (Ezra 9:4). A transgression is a sin against God's law (1 John 3:4). Their marriages caused them to sin against God's law. In this case, it was the Law of Moses. Ezra commanded them to put away these wives according to the law. Read their response with me:

"Now while Ezra was praying, and while he was confessing, weeping, and bowing down before the house of God, a very large congregation of men, women, and children assembled to him from Israel; for the people wept very bitterly. And Shechaniah the son of Jehiel, one of the sons of Elam, spoke up and said to Ezra, 'We have trespassed against our God, and have taken pagan wives from the peoples of the land; yet now there is hope in Israel in spite of this. Now therefore, let us make a covenant with our God to put away all these wives and those who have been born to them, according to the counsel of my master and of those who tremble at the commandment of our God; and let it be done according to the law. Arise, for this matter is your responsibility. We also will be with you. Be of good courage, and do it" (Ezra 10:1-4).

Let us continue reading from Ezra 10:10-13: "Then Ezra the priest stood up and said to them, 'You have transgressed and have taken pagan wives, adding to the guilt of Israel. Now therefore, make confession to the Lord God of your fathers, and do His will; separate yourselves from the peoples of the land, and from the pagan wives.' Then all the congregation answered and said with a loud voice, 'Yes! As you have said, so we must do. But there are many people; it is the season for heavy rain, and we are not able to stand outside. Nor is this the work of one or two days, for there are many of us who have transgressed in this matter.'"

They said, "...there are many of us who have transgressed in this matter." Some use this as an argument to turn a blind eye today. They say, "But there are so many people who are in an unscriptural marriage, that we cannot

170

ask them to change." This was not the attitude of Ezra or of the guilty people. You either want to serve the Lord or you don't. They decided to obey God, "And they gave their promise that they would put away their wives; and being guilty, they presented a ram of the flock as their trespass offering" (Ezra 10:19).

Read also Ezra 10:44: "All these had taken pagan wives, and some of them had wives by whom they had children." The fact that children were involved did not negate the sin. How sad it is when we drag our children into our sinful decisions and victimize them. They are the real victims here! But, when a sin is committed, that child needs to learn from their parents how to address that sin. They need to learn repentance firsthand.

Some decide to live their lives as they please. They have the same attitude that Jeremiah faced in the long ago: "As for the word that you have spoken to us in the name of the Lord, we will not listen to you! But we will certainly do whatever has gone out of our own mouth…" (Jeremiah 44:16-17).

Paul dealt with the issue of divorce as well (1 Corinthians 7:10-16). Paul begins by essentially restating the Lord's words, saying, "A wife is not to depart from her husband. But even if she does depart, let her remain unmarried or be reconciled to her husband. And a husband is not to divorce his wife" (1 Corinthians 7:10-11).

Why should they remain unmarried? Jesus has said, "Whoever divorces his wife, except for fornication, and marries another, commits adultery…" Paul was counseling them to refrain from a divorce that would lead to adultery. The guilty, departing party had no Scriptural right to remarry.

Paul adds, "If any brother has a wife who does not believe, and she is willing to live with him, let him not divorce her. And a woman who has a husband who does not believe, if he is willing to live with her, let her not divorce him" (1 Corinthians 7:12-13). Christians are not required to marry *only* because of faith. Hence, the marriage bond is not to be broken *only* because of faith.

He continues, "But if the unbeliever departs, let him depart; a brother or a sister is not under bondage in such cases. But God has called us to peace" (1 Corinthians 7:15). The case at hand is one in which a brother or sister is forsaken by a disbelieving spouse. The implication from verses twelve, thirteen, and sixteen is that they are departing because they are not pleased to dwell with a Christian spouse. This passage does not suggest a departure for any reason. It does not suggest a divorce between Christians. And, it does not suggest a marriage to a third party.

Two other possibilities remain – reconciliation and remaining unmarried (see v.11). "Bondage" herein appears to refer to a greater subjection to the disbelieving spouse than to Christ. Christians are not bound to keep the marriage covenant above the covenant they have with Christ.

REMARRIAGE

Let us now focus on the possibility of remarriage. A marriage to another by the innocent party is permitted in the case of fornication or in the case of death. Jesus has said, "And I say to you, whoever divorces his wife, except for fornication, and marries another, commits adultery; and whoever marries her who is divorced commits adultery" (Matthew 19:9). Paul has said, "A wife is bound by law as long as her husband lives; but if her husband dies, she is at liberty to be married to whom she wishes, only in the Lord" (1 Corinthians 7:39).

A marriage to another by the guilty party or without fornication being involved is adultery; for "...whoever divorces his wife, except for fornication, and marries another, commits adultery; and whoever marries her who is divorced commits adultery" (Matthew 19:9).

Adultery is a sin in which people live. "For the woman who has a husband is bound by the law to her husband as long as he lives. But if the husband dies, she is released from the law of her husband. So then if, while her husband lives, she marries another man, she will be called an adulteress; but if her husband dies, she is free from that law, so that she is no adulteress, though she has married another man" (Romans 7:2-3). How long was this woman living in adultery? The Bible says, "As long as her husband lived."

In Galatians, Paul wrote concerning the works of the flesh (Galatians 5:19-21). The very first "work of the flesh" Paul mentions is adultery. What is adultery? "Whoever divorces his wife, except for fornication, and marries another, commits adultery; and whoever marries her who is divorced commits adultery." What is the consequence for this sin? "Those who practice such things will not inherit the kingdom of God" (Galatians 5:21).

Adultery is a serious matter. Adultery makes the subject of marriage, divorce, and remarriage so serious. Men and women should marry knowing God's will on the matter, knowing their soon-to-be spouse's marital history, and that the marriage covenant is to be kept for life.

We cannot continue divorcing like we're doing. Families are being wrecked, children are victimized, and churches are devastated. We cannot continue allowing false doctrine to be taught on this subject. And we cannot continue to bury

173

our heads in the sand, remain silent, and make this the "don't ask – don't tell" policy of the church.

IN CONCLUSION

God's word can be easily understood by a willing and honest heart. Marriage is between a man and a woman (preferably faithful Christians) for life. God hates divorce. Fornication is the exception granted by Christ for a divorce. Unless a divorce occurs for the cause of fornication, any remarriage will result in adultery.

Adultery will cost you your soul – forbidding you entrance into the kingdom of heaven. Adultery is a sin. As with every sin, man must repent. Man cannot repent of this sin and continue living therein. To repent of the sin of adultery, a person must come out of that union which is causing the adultery.

It could be that someone giving attention to this lesson is currently living in adultery through an unscriptural divorce and remarriage. Let us repeat the words of Christ, "and there are eunuchs who have made themselves eunuchs for the kingdom of heaven's sake. He who is able to accept it, let him accept it" (Matthew 19:12).

THE DASH IN THE MIDDLE

I am sure that most of us know what it is like to pay a visit to a graveside. In that silent city of rest we have memorials to our loved ones. It is there that we bid our final farewell to the earthly remains of those who are dear to our hearts. It is there that we weep, we mourn, and we give an earnest heed to the sobering reality of death and the resurrection.

Concerning our mortality, at some point, we each must pay that sleeping city one last visit. I cannot tell you when that last visit will come. Only God knows. The Bible says, "It is appointed for man once to die and then the judgment" (Hebrews 9:27). I cannot tell you when that day will occur. I can only urge you not to take *today* for granted. "Do not boast about tomorrow, for you do not know what a day may bring forth" (Proverbs 27:1).

Concerning our immortality, Longfellow has well-said:

> *"Life is real! Life is earnest!*
> *And the grave is not the goal;*
> *Dust thou art, to dust returnest,*
> *Was not spoken of the soul."*

The soul of man shall live somewhere forever. Truly, "the dust will return to the earth as it was, and the spirit will return to God who gave it" (Ecclesiastes 12:7).

Through a number of ways we try to comfort ourselves through the grieving process. Flowers are usually in order. Some like to be buried alongside loved ones, maybe a spouse or their children. A great deal of ceremony usually accompanies such sad occasions. I have also noted that almost every grave has had at some point some type of marker.

Consider for a moment these markers which adorn our cemeteries. As our bodies will lie at these places awaiting the resurrection, it is likely that a marker, a tombstone of some sort, will indicate our final resting place on this earth. We're all familiar with such headstones, I believe.

Usually a person's name is listed. However, the name is not the most important marking on that piece of stone. Peter said in the presence of Cornelius, "Of a truth I perceive that God is no respecter of persons: but in every nation he that feareth Him, and worketh righteousness, is accepted with Him" (Acts 10:34-35; KJV). God is not going to save a person on the basis of who his father or mother was or the prestige of his last name. According to Peter, God shall save those who fear Him and work righteousness.

You will also find that many of these markers have an epitaph. However, these words can be rather meaningless. For instance, it could say "loving father" when the man was cold and heartless to his children. It could say "faithful Christian" to honor a person who had never obeyed the gospel. Such words can become meaningless when based on human opinions or self-conceptions. Truly, the only opinion that matters is the opinion of God.

The most important marking on any headstone is often the most overlooked. You will find it between the person's date of birth and date of death. It is that little dash in the middle. That little dash represents the sum total of a person's life. Who was he? What did he represent? What did he stand for and against? What did he believe to be true? Who did he love? Who did he serve? What were his passions? And most importantly, what did he do for the sake of his soul? Was he a servant of God or of sin?

Everyone has a choice of serving someone or something in this life. Joshua challenged the children of Israel to "choose this day whom you will serve" (Joshua 24:15). Paul asked the church at Rome, "Do you not know that to whom you present yourselves slaves to obey, you are that one's slaves whom you obey, whether of sin to death, or of obedience to righteousness?" (Romans 6:16)

Let us borrow from James and ask, "What is your life?" Are you a servant of God or of sin? Will you be a slave to sin or to righteousness? How do you want to be remembered? Perhaps we can persuade you to be a servant of God by simply comparing and contrasting the possible two lives.

THE OBITUARY OF A SERVANT OF SIN

The obituary of a lost man can be read from the pages of Scripture. The lost man can be described as "stiff-necked and uncircumcised in heart and ears" (Acts 7:51). The lost man can be described as being a stranger to the covenants of promise (Ephesians 2:12). Esau's obituary read that he was a profane person (Hebrews 12:16). The obituary of the "five-talent man" reads that he was a wicked and lazy servant (Matthew 25:26). The obituary of the rich but covetous farmer tells us that he was a fool in the sight of God (Luke 12:20).

The life lived by the servant of sin is a descending journey into eternity. While a person may enjoy some pleasures from his sins, they are not lasting. The pleasures of sin are for but a season. They are passing, even fleeting pleasures that will not endure. "By faith Moses, when he became of age, refused to be called the son of Pharaoh's daughter, choosing rather to suffer affliction with the people of God than to enjoy *the passing pleasures of sin*, esteeming the reproach of Christ greater riches than the treasures in Egypt; for he looked to the reward" (Hebrews 11:24-26). Sin not only offers no lasting pleasure, it provides no sustaining

177

fruit. Paul once asked, "What fruit did you have then in the things of which you are now ashamed? For the end of those things is death" (Romans 6:21).

One cannot enjoy the fruits of sin forever. Sin is a profitless business. You cannot win. You cannot succeed – not in this life or in the life to come. Someone might say he can succeed by sinning his way into a fortune. Possibly, this is true. But, I can assure you it will be the emptiest fortune he can imagine. Not only that, but he would have given up a prize far more precious than gold and silver to attain it – his immortal soul.

The servant of sin has no hope in the future. John writes, "Do not love the world or the things in the world. If anyone loves the world, the love of the Father is not in him. For all that is in the world the lust of the flesh, the lust of the eyes, and the pride of life is not of the Father but is of the world. And the world is passing away, and the lust of it; but he who does the will of God abides forever" (1 John 2:15-17). If you are hitching your wagon to the ways of the world, you are going to be led down a dead-end road.

The servant of sin has no hope in this world or the world to come. When the Ephesians were "dead in trespasses and sins" (Ephesians 2:1), walking "according to the course of this world, according to the prince of the power of the air, the spirit who now works in the sons of disobedience" (Ephesians 2:2), they were "without Christ, being aliens from the commonwealth of Israel and strangers from the covenants of promise, having no hope and without God in the world" (Ephesians 2:12).

Paul has painted a pretty sad picture, but it gets worse. You see, to this point we have been discussing the woes that befall the servant of sin in this life. Now let us turn our attention to the life beyond.

The servant of sin has no inheritance beyond death. "Now the works of the flesh are evident, which are: adultery, fornication, uncleanness, licentiousness, idolatry, sorcery, hatred, contentions, jealousies, outbursts of wrath, selfish ambitions, dissensions, heresies, envy, murders, drunkenness, revelries, and the like; of which I tell you beforehand, just as I also told you in time past, that those who practice such things will not inherit the kingdom of God" (Galatians 5:19-21).

The servant of sin has no mercy in the world to come. In the sixteenth chapter of Luke, we read of a certain rich man who was a servant to sin in this life, but in the life to come he is crying out, "Father Abraham, have mercy on me, and send Lazarus that he may dip the tip of his finger in water and cool my tongue; for I am tormented in this flame" (Luke 16:24). Father Abraham's reply will send a chill down your spine. "Son, remember that in your lifetime you received your good things, and likewise Lazarus evil things; but now he is comforted and you are tormented." The rich servant of sin was not even granted a fingertip full of water in those flames. He was told to remember. He might as well start liking it. He was as comforted as he would ever be. He had only just opened his eyes to that place and already he had his fill. He didn't want any more of it. He would give anything for one more chance to give up his sins and surrender to God. He would have traded all his fortunes and gladly given his place at the table of ease and splendor for Lazarus' place at the gate, if only he could. But it was too late for that. He had lived his life according to the passing pleasures of sin and now he was going to have to live with the consequences of his selfishness.

Vividly pictured in the sixteenth chapter of Luke is a rich man tormented in flames. He didn't ask for a glass or even a thimble full of water. He only wanted a taste to cool his tongue. He should have thought about that before he died. He should have prepared himself for death. He should have chosen to live his life in service to God. He wanted to serve Satan, sin, and self but now look at him. Why not ask Satan to get some water? Where is the father of lies in all of this? What is he able to offer the rich man now?

THE OBITUARY OF A SERVANT OF GOD

The obituary of a servant of God may very well read like that of Enoch who walked with God (Genesis 5:24). It could read like Abraham's, who was called the "friend of God" (James 2:23). Or, he may simply be called a wise and faithful servant (Matthew 25:21, 23).

Speaking as a child of God, Paul once said, "If in this life only we have hope in Christ, we are of all men the most pitiable" (1 Corinthians 15:19). How sad it would be to know that this world is as good as it will ever get. The child of God has more than that. The child of God has the hope of eternal life "which God, who cannot lie, promised before time began" (Titus 1:2). While the servant of sin is forever ruined and cursed by sin, the servant of God is forever blessed by God.

Every child of God has the promise of eternal salvation. Christ is the "author of eternal salvation to all who obey Him" (Hebrews 5:9). The servant of God has the promise of an eternal home. Jesus promises, "Let not your heart be troubled; you believe in God, believe also in Me. In My Father's house are many mansions; if it were not so, I would have told you. I go to prepare a place for you. And if I go and prepare a place for you, I will come again and receive you to Myself; that where I am, there you may be also" (John 14:1-3). And, God's people are promised an eternal inheritance. Jesus has promised these words to His faithful children at the final judgment: "Come, you blessed of My Father, inherit the kingdom prepared for you from the foundation of the world" (Matthew 25:34).

The servant of sin has no inheritance. The child of God has an inheritance that has been in the making even before the foundation of the world. The servant of sin is living a descending life. The servant of God is living an ascending life. The child of God can live an abundant life here and now (John 10:10). He can enjoy spiritual growth (2 Peter 1:5-11; 2 Peter 3:18). And, when his life of spiritual prosperity and blessedness draws to its close, he can enjoy a heavenly home and eternal life in glory.

IN CONCLUSION

Having studied these facts from God's word, let me borrow a question from Peter and ask you, "What manner of persons ought you to be in holy conduct and godliness?" (2 Peter 3:11) Will you choose to live or die eternally? A servant of righteousness is promised a resurrection of reward. A servant of sin is promised a resurrection of damnation (John 5:29). Which will it be for you? "How shall we escape if we neglect so great a salvation?"

With a sense of urgency, Paul wrote to his brethren in Rome saying, "And do this, knowing the time, that now it is high time to awake out of sleep; for now our salvation is nearer than when we first believed. The night is far spent, the day is at hand. Therefore let us cast off the works of darkness, and let us put on the armor of light. Let us walk properly, as in the day, not in revelry and drunkenness, not in licentiousness and lewdness, not in strife and envy. But put on the Lord Jesus Christ, and make no provision for the flesh, to fulfill its lusts" (Romans 13:11-14).

Decide for yourself what you want that dash in the middle to signify on your tombstone. We implore and invite you to "Seek the Lord while He may be found, call upon Him while He is near" (Isaiah 55:6). "And now why are you waiting? Arise and be baptized, and wash away your sins, calling on the name of the Lord" (Acts 22:16).

A TWELVE-STEP PROGRAM THAT IS GUARANTEED

I understand that there is a twelve-step program that can be taken to help people overcome substance addiction. I'm thankful that people care enough about their loved ones and about their own condition that they would seek the necessary help in such situations. I understand that the goal for the program is sobriety. I also understand that it works for some people and not for others. Usually, success is determined by the desire of the one seeking the help. This lesson has to do with a twelve-step program as well. If you'll look to the Holy Scriptures, you will find that God has given us a twelve-step program with the goals being both for this life and the life to come. If we will follow this twelve-step program, we are promised that we will be fruitful in our knowledge of the word and an entrance will be supplied "abundantly into the everlasting kingdom of our Lord and Savior Jesus Christ" (2 Peter 1:11).

Our steps include five steps which lead us to the church, and seven steps that must be taken while living as a child of God to lead us to heaven. We have five steps from sinner to saint and seven steps from the church to heaven. When these twelve steps are taken faithfully as God has taught us, we are promised that we shall never fall and an entrance into the eternal kingdom of heaven shall be abundantly supplied.

STEP ONE: HEAR THE GOSPEL

The first step is to hear the gospel. To make sure that the gospel could be heard by the lost, our Lord commanded us, "Go into all the world and preach the gospel to every creature" (Mark 16:15). The gospel must be preached faithfully and heard with humility in order for sinners to obey it.

When we speak of "hearing the word," we are speaking as James spoke, of "receiving the word." Man must "receive with meekness the implanted word, which is able to save your souls" (James 1:21). We must take heed how we hear and receive the word. A true, biblical faith depends on *what* we hear and *how* we hear it.

I say that because not everyone receives the word with meekness and humility. Some will get mad at you for mentioning the Lord's name. Regrettably, some will hear the word of God with contempt and malice in their hearts. They never get past the first step. No one can force them into taking another step. It is not sufficient to stop at hearing. James said you ought to be "doers of the word, and not hearers only, deceiving yourselves" (James 1:22). Hearing must be mixed with faith (Hebrews 4:2).

STEP TWO: BELIEVE THE GOSPEL

One must believe the message he has heard. This is our second step. One must have the faith that hearing the gospel produces. "So then faith comes by hearing, and hearing by the word of God" (Romans 10:17).

Faith is the result of properly receiving the word of God; and without faith a person will never be saved. "Without faith it is impossible to please Him, for he who comes to God must believe that He is, and that He rewards those who diligently seek Him" (Hebrews 11:6). That person without faith will never be pleasing to God. However, if that person decides to believe the gospel, he must not stop at believing. He still has three more steps to get into Christ. He still has ten more steps to get to heaven. Just because he believes is no reason to quit climbing. In fact, it is all the more reason to keep climbing!

STEP THREE: REPENT OF SINS

The next step is repentance. Repentance is turning from sin and turning to God. It is a change of will which produces a change of life. Repentance can be motivated by godly sorrow over sin (2 Corinthians 7:10-11). It can also be motivated by acknowledging the goodness of God (Romans 2:4). Only when man is properly motivated will he repent. And only when man repents will he be saved. Jesus said, "Except you repent, you shall all likewise perish" (Luke 13:3, 5). God is commanding all men to repent (Acts 17:30-31). He is longsuffering in giving man an opportunity to repent (2 Peter 3:9).

If a person is unwilling to repent, he is simply stuck on the second step. He has quit climbing. He is unwilling to turn from his sins in order to walk with God. God is willing to help him. God is willing to save him. But the impenitent person is unwilling to receive help and to be saved. He would rather remain in his sins and be lost than to forsake his sins and be saved. There are three things that God has always required of sinful man – faith, repentance, and obedience.

STEP FOUR: CONFESS FAITH IN CHRIST OF SINS

With a heart full of trusting faith and penitence, man is free to confess Christ as the Son of God. Confession is not something we do one time and then forget about it. We are to continue hearing, believing, repenting of sin, and confessing Christ every day of our lives.

However, there is a special confession to be made before one can go any farther in this twelve-step program. It is the confession that was made by the Ethiopian eunuch prior to his baptism when he said, "I believe that Jesus Christ is the Son of God" (Acts 8:37).

STEP FIVE: BAPTISM INTO CHRIST

When we take these five steps – hear, believe, repent, confess, and baptism – the Lord will forgive our sins and save us by His grace. It has been this way since the church began and it will continue to be this way until Christ comes again.

Not only are we saved by grace through faith (Ephesians 2:8), but we are also added to the Lord's church. We do not join the church of our choice. According to the Scriptures, God adds the saved to His church (Acts 2:47).

He adds us to the church when we obey the gospel (2 Thessalonians 2:14). We are taken from the kingdom of darkness and added to the kingdom of His dear Son (Colossians 1:13).

All of this happens when we are baptized into Christ for the remission of sins. Read with me from Acts 2:38-41: "Then Peter said to them, 'Repent, and let every one of you be baptized in the name of Jesus Christ for the remission of sins; and you shall receive the gift of the Holy Spirit. For the promise is to you and to your children, and to all who are afar off, as many as the Lord our God will call.' And with many other words he testified and exhorted them, saying, 'Be saved from this perverse generation.' Then those who gladly received his word were baptized; and that day about three thousand souls were added to them."

You have just read that these souls were baptized in the name of Christ. Christ fully authorizes this act. They were baptized for the remission or forgiveness of their sins, in order to save themselves from that perverse generation.

They gladly received the gospel message. They heard the gospel preached, believed it, repented of their sins, and were baptized in the name of Christ. Upon so doing, the Lord

186

added those three thousand souls to His church that day. Once we have been added to the church, it is time to grow as babes in Christ. Having been saved by grace through faith, Christians must live with a holy purpose, even as Christ's workmanship who have been created unto good works (Ephesians 2:10).

Peter teaches us how to do this in 2 Peter 1:5-11. He is going to provide our seven steps to heaven. Observe, "But also for this very reason (that is, having escaped the pollution of the world (v.4), giving all diligence, add to your faith virtue, to virtue knowledge, to knowledge self-control, to self-control perseverance, to perseverance godliness, to godliness brotherly kindness, and to brotherly kindness love. For if these things are yours and abound, you will be neither barren nor unfruitful in the knowledge of our Lord Jesus Christ. For he who lacks these things is shortsighted, even to blindness, and has forgotten that he was purged from his old sins. Therefore, brethren, be even more diligent to make your calling and election sure, for if you do these things you will never stumble; for so an entrance will be supplied to you abundantly into the everlasting kingdom of our Lord and Savior Jesus Christ."

STEP SIX: VIRTUE

As members of the Lord's spiritual body, His church, we must add to our faith "virtue." Virtue is the first step required of a Christian. Virtue is simply the determination to do that which is right. Virtue is moral excellence. Christians are called to moral excellence. "Except your righteousness exceeds the righteousness of the scribes and Pharisees you will by no means enter the kingdom of heaven" (Matthew 5:20). "For the grace of God that brings salvation has appeared to all men, teaching us that, denying ungodliness and worldly lusts, we should live soberly, righteously, and godly in the present age" (Titus 2:11-12).

Virtue is a word seldom heard anymore to describe anyone. Nevertheless, it is the first quality that must be added to our faith. We must be holy for God is holy (1 Peter 1:16) and be perfect as our Father in heaven is perfect (Matthew 5:48). We are Christ's representatives and it makes perfect sense as to why this step is essential to making heaven our home.

STEP SEVEN: KNOWLEDGE

The seventh step is knowledge. God desires for His children to grow in the grace and knowledge of the Lord (2 Peter 3:18). It takes determination to study and it takes study to gain knowledge (2 Timothy 2:15).

A lack of knowledge will cause God's people to perish today as surely as it did in Hosea's day (Hosea 4:6). Yet, virtue must first exist before there can be growth in the knowledge of the word. If we are lacking knowledge, we must first be lacking virtue – moral excellence, determination to do that which is right. How can we study, learn, and gain knowledge if we have not first determined to grow in Christ?

Knowledge comes by searching the Scriptures (John 5:39). It takes long, taxing hours to learn God's word as we should. "Much study is wearisome to the flesh" (Ecclesiastes 12:12). To be a good Bible student a person will have to devote a lifetime of diligent effort. I remember a teacher of mine once telling a story about getting to visit with an older, learned teacher of God's word when he was a young man. The young man said to the older, "I'd give twenty years of my life to know the Bible like you know it." To which the older man replied, "You will give a lot more than that."

STEP EIGHT: SELF-CONTROL

Having grown and being determined to grow in our knowledge, we must begin to apply what we learn. We must first work on "self." "Remove the plank in your own eye." Thus, our eighth step is "self-control."

We must learn self-control in our temperament and when facing temptations. We must have self-control to be able to resist the devil and draw near to God (James 4:6-10). We must grow in wisdom and virtue to the point that we can strongly resist those situations that provoke us to anger and to sin.

How essential is self-control to the salvation of the soul! The book of James is a great discourse on the need for self-control. We must endure temptation (James 1:12 ff.). We must control our tongues (James 3:2 ff.). We must control our thoughts (James 3:13 ff.). We must control our desires (James 4:1 ff.). We must control our finances (James 5:1 ff.). And we must control our attitudes (James 5:7 ff.).

The Christian who exercises self-control in these ways is an example to all. But, the man who lacks self-control is viewed as a hypocrite.

STEP NINE: PERSEVERANCE

We add to our self-control perseverance. Perseverance is the ninth step. The idea is that of endurance. We must keep the faith.

Jesus said, "In your patience (you) possess your souls" (Luke 21:19). We must be patient and endure in tribulations (Romans 12:12). Of course, we'll never be able to endure this way if we do not first have self-control.

Do you see how these steps work together? When we are able to deal with troubles from within (self-control), we will be better able to deal with troubles from without (perseverance). The meek shall inherit the earth (Matthew 5:5).

STEP TEN: GODLINESS

We have dealt with our view of self, our view of trials, and now we are dealing with our view of God. Our next step is godliness. *Godliness* is a humble reverence toward God which affects our disposition toward life.

Christians are to approach God in humble reverence and deep piety. He is not our "Daddy" or "the Big Man upstairs." He is our Holy Father and for that we should be grateful. We must learn to serve Him with "reverence and godly fear" (Hebrews 12:28). When we assemble to worship we are assembling into His presence. Let us respect it as such.

Christians are to approach life with a godly spirit. We are to conduct ourselves in "all holy conversation (manner of life) and godliness" (2 Peter 3:11). "Godliness with contentment is great gain" (1 Timothy 6:6). Godliness is one of the things a man of God is to pursue, along with righteousness, faith, love, patience, and gentleness (1 Timothy 6:11).

Godliness can be described as "God-like-ness." It is to view the world as He views the world, to judge matters of right and wrong as He judges them, and to implement the moral purity exemplified in the life of His only-begotten Son.

STEP ELEVEN: BROTHERLY LOVE

The eleventh step to heaven concerns our view of brethren. It is brotherly love. Brotherly love must continue (Hebrews 13:1).

Let me say that this is not always an easy thing to do. I am convinced that the best friends I have on earth are certain brothers and sisters I have in Christ. I am convinced that the best people I have known were faithful Christians. And, I am convinced that ministering and preaching for these souls is the greatest work on earth.

Nevertheless, I am also convinced that some brethren have just enough religion to make others miserable. Some brethren will surely try to ruin the goodness and sweetness of our fellowship for everyone. It is baffling to me, personally, how a person can be so unloving, unmerciful, and unkind and then sing "O' how I love Jesus." The Bible teaches us that if we truly love Him, we will love one another (1 John 3-4). Jesus has said, "By this all men shall know that you are My disciples, if you have love for one another" (John 13:35). We are to love one another with a pure heart, fervently (1 Peter 1:22).

Brotherly love ought not to be as challenging as some have made it out to be. Indeed, some people cause joy wherever they go, while others cause joy whenever they leave. I wish we would all be more considerate of one another. The writer of Hebrews has said, "Let us consider one another, to provoke unto love and good works" (Hebrews 10:24). We ought to be provoking one another to love and good works, not envy, strife, anger, malice, and backbiting. God has put us together to help, not hinder, one another. God's plan for the church is that we edify (build up) one another in love (Ephesians 4:15), not tear down, bite, and devour.

STEP TWELVE: LOVE

The twelfth step involves our view of the world. It is love in general. Without love, none of us will make it to heaven. Love is the greatest of all emotions (1 Corinthians 13:13). "Love suffers long and is kind; love does not envy;

love does not parade itself, is not puffed up; does not behave rudely, does not seek its own, is not provoked, thinks no evil; does not rejoice in iniquity, but rejoices in the truth; bears all things, believes all things, hopes all things, endures all things. Love never fails...." (1 Corinthians 13:4-8).

To love is to be like God, for God is love (1 John 4:8). Let us love the Lord, His word, His church, and our fellow man.

IN CONCLUSION

Beloved, this is a twelve-step program that's guaranteed! "For if these things are yours and abound, you will be neither barren nor unfruitful in the knowledge of our Lord Jesus Christ." Never quit climbing. "For he who lacks these things is shortsighted, even to blindness, and has forgotten that he was purged from his old sins." If we do these things, we shall never fall, but if we don't do these things, yea indeed we have fallen already. The result of this climb is life eternal. That's my goal and I hope it is your goal too.

Let's help each other to make heaven our home. "Therefore, brethren, be even more diligent to make your calling and election sure, for if you do these things you will never stumble; for so an entrance will be supplied to you abundantly into the everlasting kingdom of our Lord and Savior Jesus Christ."

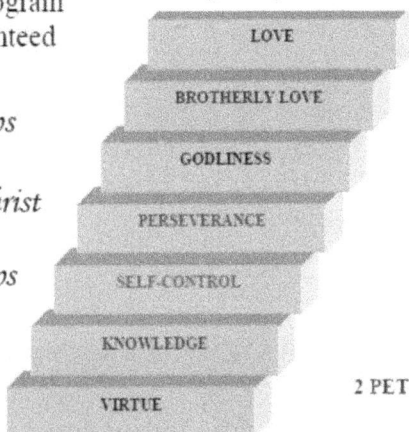

A 12 Step Program
That's Guaranteed

*Five Steps
to the
Church of Christ
and

Seven Steps
to

Heaven*

"*Entrance into the
Everlasting
Kingdom of our Lord...*"

LOVE

BROTHERLY LOVE

GODLINESS

PERSEVERANCE

SELF-CONTROL

KNOWLEDGE

VIRTUE

2 PETER 1:5-11

ACTS 2:47; COLOSIANS 1:13
CHURCH
OF
CHRIST
MATTHEW 16:13-18

Keep Growing

&

Keep Climbing

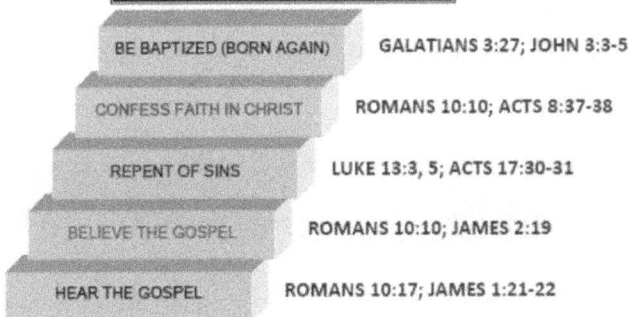

BE BAPTIZED (BORN AGAIN)   GALATIANS 3:27; JOHN 3:3-5

CONFESS FAITH IN CHRIST   ROMANS 10:10; ACTS 8:37-38

REPENT OF SINS   LUKE 13:3, 5; ACTS 17:30-31

BELIEVE THE GOSPEL   ROMANS 10:10; JAMES 2:19

HEAR THE GOSPEL   ROMANS 10:17; JAMES 1:21-22

RESTORING THE ERRING

"Brethren, if a man is overtaken in any trespass, you who are spiritual restore such a one in a spirit of gentleness, considering yourself lest you also be tempted. Bear one another's burdens, and so fulfill the law of Christ" (Galatians 6:1-2).

With this particular lesson, let's begin by analyzing a few of the words and phrases used by Paul in this passage. Paul said, "If a man is overtaken in any *trespass...*" What is a "trespass?" To be clear, to trespass is sin. To sin is to trespass or "transgress" the law of God (1 John 3:4). It is to go beyond the limits of God's commands and to violate His will.

Notice also that this sin has *overtaken* the brother. The sin has taken control of the man so as to direct his thoughts, words, or deeds. It is not merely that the brother has sin which he needs to confess to God, for every Christian has such a need (1 John 1:8-10). The sin of this man have subdued his spirit and subjugated his soul so as to mar his influence for good and to cause him to wander from the fold of God. We should regard this brother as one who needs to be restored to his former place. His sin has caused him to defect from the truth and divorce himself from Christ.

With concern for such a brother, Paul's fixes his attention upon the spiritual ones of the church. To be spiritual is to be *spiritually-minded.* A line of demarcation can be drawn between the spiritually-minded and the carnally-minded by observing their willingness to restore a fallen brother. The carnally-minded man will question the brother's sincerity. The carnally-minded man will refuse to forgive. The carnally-minded man will hold a grudge want to exact vengeance! If you would like to learn who are the spiritually-minded and who are the carnally-minded in a congregation, just observe how that treat a penitent brother.

To *restore* is to put that brother or sister in the order of the former condition, even with all the fullness of Christian fellowship that once existed. When we forgive we let go of the desire to get revenge and promise that the matter will not be brought up again, or allowed to be a barrier. When we forgive we are putting the past behind us and moving on with life.

The *burdens* mentioned by Paul are the burdens sin has brought upon the wayward brother. Sin can take quite a toll on a person's life. Sometimes the sin can be so serious and so grievous that the wayward brother will need considerable help from his church family in order to rebuild his life. In such cases we are called to "Bear one another's burdens, and so fulfill the law of Christ."

The *law of Christ* is the new covenant of the Son of God. It is the gospel, the law of faith, the law of liberty, even the commandments of our Lord. When we restore the wayward in a spirit of gentleness, we are obeying the commandments of our Savior. Is such forgiveness as is required from this passage not the "Golden Rule" in action?

In the midst of these instructions Paul teaches us to restore the wayward "in a spirit of gentleness, considering yourself lest you also be tempted." Two ideas stand out to me when I read this instruction. (1) A haughty man can never bear the spiritual burdens of the weak. He is incapable of manifesting the necessary gentleness and humility required to encourage and restore anyone. (2) We must consider ourselves, our attitudes, and our actions when a brother needs our forgiveness. It *does* indeed matter to God how we treat a penitent person. We must forgive because God has forgiven us (Matthew 18:21-35). We must forgive so that we might gain our brother (Matthew 18:15; 2 Corinthians 2:7-8). We must forgive so that we might continue to be forgiven (Mark 11:25-26; James 2:13). And we forgive so that we might be freed from the anger, resentment, and bitterness we would otherwise have (see Ephesians 4:31-32). If we refuse to forgive, we will be consumed by bitterness and fall into the snare of the devil ourselves.

OUR FELLOWSHIP IN CHRIST

In order to illustrate our fellowship in Christ, simply draw or imagine a circle. Inside this circle, on the left side, write: "Individual." Then, draw an arrow toward the center and write: "God." Complete it by drawing an arrow over to the right hand side and write: "Church." Make sure your arrows point in both directions, toward the church and toward the individual on the sides and toward God in the center. This is the fellowship we have in Christ (1 Corinthians 1:9). Christians have fellowship with one another *through* or *because of* the fellowship we have with God in Christ (1 John 1:3).

The apostle John said, "If we say that we have fellowship with Him, and walk in darkness, we lie and do not practice the truth. But if we walk in the light as He is in the light, *we have fellowship with one another*, and the blood of Jesus Christ His Son cleanses us from all sin" (1 John 1:6-7).

Faithful Christians are in fellowship with God. Being in fellowship with God requires walking in the light and results in continued fellowship with all others also in fellowship with God. The blessing inherent with such providential fellowship remains: "the blood of Jesus Christ His Son cleanses us from all sin."

WHY ARE THEY IN ERROR?

The erring brother has left this circle. By being overtaken in his sins, he has walked out on the fellowship he had with God and the church, which is in Christ. God did not leave him. God will never leave us or forsake us (Hebrews 13:5). The wayward child left God. The erring child of God has literally divorced himself from the most sacred of all his relationships. Through the deceitfulness of sin, he has departed from the living God (Hebrews 3:12).

If we sever ourselves from this fellowship with Him, we are severing ourselves from the church. If we choose to sever ourselves from the church, the body, we are also choosing to sever ourselves from the Lord, the Head of the body. We cannot have Christ without the church or the church without Christ.

When Christians "depart from the living God" it is because at some point they have left their first love (Revelation 2:4). I do not believe the typical erring brother conscientiously determined to leave the Lord. I believe in most instances it started by becoming slack in some biblical responsibility. Perhaps they became increasingly negligent in their worship to God. Maybe they gradually fell away from good Bible study habits or personal prayer. Before you know it, they are nowhere to be found at the church's assemblies.

The wayward brother has left his first love and must remember, repent, and return (Revelation 2:4 ff.). His religion may have grown lukewarm (Revelation 3:16). He loves the world and is enthralled by the lust of the flesh, the lust of the eyes and the pride of life (1 John 2:15). He is walking disorderly (2 Thessalonians 3:6). He is not growing in faith and knowledge as he should (Hebrews 5:11). Rather, he is sinning willfully, trampling beneath his feet the blood of Christ (Hebrews 10:26 ff.).

For some wayward brethren, their faith is more like a roller coaster than anything else. Their spiritual fervor is full of extreme highs and very depressing lows. Oftentimes, they cannot escape their lows until they begin walking disorderly. They may begin frequenting places no godly-minded person would dare to enter. They may begin practicing a "secret sin." Rather than feel like a "Sunday morning hypocrite" they simply choose to forsake the Lord. Sadly, marriages will end during such low periods. Children will be neglected. And in some cases, churches will even split over a controversy such an extreme low has caused.

Rather than repent of their wickedness, and seek Christ's help (the best friend they'll ever have), they become friends with the world and set themselves at enmity with God (James 4:4). Usually, they turn their backs to many of their Christian friends and seek the approval of people who "know not God, nor the works which He has done."

WHY DO THEY NEED TO BE RESTORED?

The wayward Christian will foolishly exchange his soul for what amounts to a brief, reckless walk in darkness. He will shipwreck his faith and even the faith of others (1 Timothy 1:19-20), while trampling beneath his feet the Son of God, even crucifying Him afresh and putting Him to an open shame (Hebrews 6:6).

The erring brother is not just entangled again, but overcome by the pollutions of the world (2 Peter 2:20). Is it any wonder the latter end is worse for them than the beginning? Peter said, "For it would have been better for them not to have known the way of righteousness, than having known it, to turn from the holy commandment delivered to them." It would have been better for that person to have died never knowing Christ, than to die having forsaken Him.

Damage has not only been done to the relationship an erring Christian has with God, but this damage extends to his brethren. He cannot enjoy fellowship with those in the light while he is walking in darkness. A person cannot have fellowship with light and darkness at the same time. He must choose to live in the light or in the darkness.

While the wayward brother is in fellowship with the world, he is at enmity with God (James 4:4). He is despising the Spirit of grace (Hebrews 10:29). He is practicing a sin unto death (1 John 5:16). You realize that we are not even permitted to pray for his forgiveness until and unless he repents. He is caught up in the works of the flesh, and to die in that condition is to forfeit the kingdom of heaven (Galatians 5:19-21).

It is because this wayward child is in such dire circumstances, that we must seek to "restore such a one in a spirit of gentleness." We must encourage such a one to return to his Father. He is going to have to return and he can only return by repenting of the sins which took him away. The wayward brother cannot be restored while his devotion is to his sins. Just as the Prodigal Son, he must repent of these sins and return to God (Luke 15:11 ff.).

WHEN DOES RESTORATION OCCUR?

Only if the erring child decides to return to his spiritual home, can things be made right with His Father, and with his brethren. God does not compromise with an erring child about his sins, and neither can the church. If he chooses not to repent and to return to the church, the church is instructed to withdraw from him (Titus 3:10). But before that should happen, every effort must be made to restore the wayward and to save a soul from death.

In order for restoration to occur, the wayward brother must be converted from the error of his way (James 5:19-20). The erring brother must repent of his sins confess them to God. Only until he repents, can he be restored. And when he does repent, we must reaffirm our love to him (2 Corinthians 2:8). Just as the church cannot extend fellowship to someone not in fellowship with God, the church cannot withhold fellowship to someone in fellowship with God. When the wayward brother makes things right with God, he makes things right with the church.

WHO RESTORES THE WAYWARD?

Restoration is twofold. God must restore the erring child and the church must restore the erring brother. In Galatians 6:1-2, Paul is teaching us about the church's responsibility to the penitent brother. Yet, there are many other passages which teach us about God's role in forgiving the wayward. The church cannot "clear" a person of his sins unless God has cleansed that person of his sins. The church does not have authority to grant something God has not granted. Sadly, many congregations choose to bury their heads in the sand and permit a person to live in sin while extending fellowship to them. Brethren, *this ought not to be*. Only when God restores a person are we commanded to restore.

HOW CAN WE BETTER RESTORE THE WAYWARD?

The erring brother must be warned (1 Thessalonians 5:14). Use compassion or fear if you must (Jude 22-23). But, warn the erring! Do not count him as an enemy, but admonish him as a brother (2 Thessalonians 3:15). He is still our brother in Christ. He is one of God's, but he must be reclaimed.

Go to the brother and talk to him. If he doesn't hear you, take others with you when you return. If you must withdraw from him in an effort to save his soul, withdraw (Matthew 18:15-17; 1 Corinthians 5). When the brother does repent, forgive him and restore him in a spirit of gentleness and love.

IN CONCLUSION

In conclusion, let us imagine how our congregations would increase in number if we could restore our erring brethren. How many more spouses, children, and prospects for conversion could we gain? By seeking to restore the erring as we should, we are hoping to save a soul from death as well as build up the body of Christ.

Why is this lesson such an important lesson? Why must the erring be restored? Why can we not just accept them in their sins? Each of these questions can be answered with one verse: "Be holy for I am holy" (1 Peter 1:16). Beloved, we represent God on this earth and that should matter to us. We are called to a higher standard. Rather than ignore the sins which have taken them away from us, we should desire more than anything to restore the erring and help bear their spiritual burdens. Let us tearfully plead with the erring, even now. Come home.

Restoring the Erring – Galatians 6:1-3

Why are they in error?
Hebrews 13:5
Hebrews 3:12-13

"Be Ye Holy"
1 Peter 1:16

Fellowship in Christ
1 Corinthians 1:9
1 John 1:3, 7

Christian ⟷ God ⟷ Church

Gal. 6:1
Rev. 2:4
1 Jn. 2:15
2 Th. 3:6
Heb. 5:11
Heb. 10:26

Why do they need to be restored?
Fellowship with the World
James 4:4; 1 Jn. 1:6; Heb. 10:29
2 Peter 2:20-22; 2 Th. 3:10-12
1 John 5:16; Galatians 5:19-21

Luke 15:11 ff.
Rev. 2:5

How can we better restore the wayward?
1 Th. 5:14
2 Th. 3:15
Matt. 18:15-17
1 Cor. 5:1-13
2 Corinthians 2:1-8

Who restores?
Acts 8:18-24
Galatians 6:1-3

When does restoration occur?
James 5:19-20; 1 Jn. 1:9; 2 Cor. 7:10

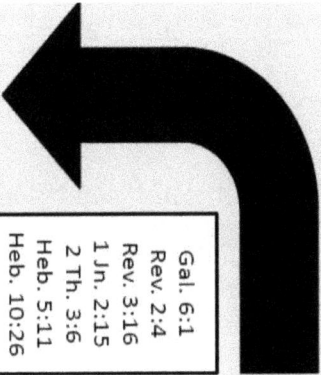

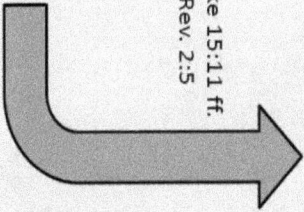

203

CHOOSE YOU THIS DAY

Sacred history teaches us that Joshua was one the great leaders of his people. His rise to prominence was the result of his obedience to the instructions of Almighty God. Joshua was a man who was willing, more than anything else in life, to trust in the Lord. Here was a man who took comfort, believed, and trusted with all of his heart in the promises of God. His obedience to God caused his campaign and conquest of the land of Canaan to be decisive and impressive.

The groundwork was laid for Joshua's success, as the mantle of Moses fell upon him, when God said to Joshua: "No man shall be able to stand before you all the days of your life; as I was with Moses, so I will be with you. I will not leave you nor forsake you. Be strong and of good courage, for to this people you shall divide as an inheritance the land which I swore to their fathers to give them. Only be strong and very courageous, that you may observe to do according to all the law which Moses My servant commanded you; do not turn from it to the right hand or to the left, that you may prosper wherever you go. This Book of the Law shall not depart from your mouth, but you shall meditate in it day and night, that you may observe to do according to all that is written in it. For then you will make your way prosperous, and then you will have good success. Have I not commanded you? Be strong and of good courage; do not be afraid, nor be dismayed, for the Lord your God is with you wherever you go" (Joshua 1:5-7).

Joshua took this message to heart and lived by it. Moreover, as any good leader would do, he was sure to communicate the importance of this message to his people. In chapter twenty-three of the book of Joshua, we learn of wise, old Joshua, well-stricken in age, calling "for all Israel, for their elders, for their heads, for their judges, and for their offic-ers" (Joshua 23:2). Once they were assembled, Joshua said unto them:

"I am old, advanced in age. You have seen all that the Lord your God has done to all these nations because of you, for the Lord your God is He who has fought for you. See, I have divided to you by lot these nations that remain, to be an in-heritance for your tribes, from the Jordan, with all the na-tions that I have cut off, as far as the Great Sea westward. And the Lord your God will expel them from before you and drive them out of your sight. So you shall possess their land, as the Lord your God has promised you. Therefore be very courageous to keep and to do all that is written in the Book of the Law of Moses, lest you turn aside from it to the right hand or to the left, and lest you go among these nations, these who remain among you. You shall not make mention of the name of their gods, nor cause anyone to swear by them; you shall not serve them nor bow down to them, but you shall hold fast to the Lord your God, as you have done to this day. For the Lord has driven out from before you great and strong nations; but as for you, no one has been able to stand against you to this day. One man of you shall chase a thousand, for the Lord your God is He who fights for you, as He has promised you. Therefore take diligent heed to yourselves, that you love the Lord your God. Or else, if in-deed you do go back, and cling to the remnant of these na-tions these that remain among you and make marriages with them, and go in to them and they to you, know for certain that the Lord your God will no longer drive out these nations from before you. But they shall be snares and traps to you, and scourges on your sides and thorns in your eyes, until you perish from this good land which the Lord your God has given you. Behold, this day I am going the way of all the earth. And you know in all your hearts and in all your souls that not one thing has failed of all the good things which the Lord your God spoke concerning you. All have come to pass for you, and not one word of them has failed. Therefore it shall come to pass, that as all the good things have come upon you which the Lord your God promised you, so the Lord will bring upon you all harmful things, until He has destroyed you from this good land which the Lord your God has given you. When you have transgressed the covenant of the Lord your God, which He commanded you, and have gone and served other gods, and bowed down to them, then the anger of the Lord will burn against you, and you shall perish quickly from the good land which He has given you" (Joshua 23:2-16).

Joshua would also gather all of the tribes to Shechem and speak to all the people a great and lasting message. It is the conclusion of this message that we remember most of all. Joshua exhorted the people by saying:

"Now therefore, fear the Lord, serve Him in sincerity and in truth, and put away the gods which your fathers served on the other side of the River and in Egypt. Serve the Lord! And if it seems evil to you to serve the Lord, choose for yourselves this day whom you will serve, whether the gods which your fathers served that were on the other side of the River, or the gods of the Amorites, in whose land you dwell. But as for me and my house, we will serve the Lord" (Joshua 24:14-15).

The people answered Joshua in one accord, saying:

"Far be it from us that we should forsake the Lord to serve other gods; for the Lord our God is He who brought us and our fathers up out of the land of Egypt, from the house of bondage, who did those great signs in our sight, and preserved us in all the way that we went and among all the people through whom we passed. And the Lord drove out from before us all the people, even the Amorites who dwelt in the land. We also will serve the Lord, for He is our God" (Joshua 24:16-18). And again, "The Lord our God we will serve, and His voice we will obey" (Joshua 24:24).

"So the people served the Lord all the days of Joshua, and all the days of the elders who outlived Joshua, who had seen all the great works of the Lord which He had done for Israel. Now Joshua the son of Nun, the servant of the Lord, died when he was one hundred and ten years old" (Judges 2:7-8).

It was to be the last great generation of God's people for many years, as:

"When all that generation had been gathered to their fathers, another generation arose after them who did not know the Lord nor the work which He had done for Israel. Then the children of Israel did evil in the sight of the Lord, and served the Baals; and they forsook the Lord God of their fathers, who had brought them out of the land of Egypt; and they followed other gods from among the gods of the people who were all around them, and they bowed down to them; and they provoked the Lord to anger. They forsook the Lord and served Baal and the Ashtoreths. And the anger of the Lord was hot against Israel. So He delivered them into the hands of plunderers who despoiled them; and He sold them into the hands of their enemies all around, so that they could no longer stand before their enemies" (Judges 2:10-14).

Joshua's exhortation to "choose you this day" applies to every generation, even our own. In the case of Israel, all it took was one generation of disobedient people to initiate a long and vexed history of idolatry that would ultimately culminate in being removed from the land of promise and subjected to Babylonian captivity. Man has made similar decisions today. Every one of us faces a similar choice. We must choose who we will serve. The temptations and the false gods may be different, but the principle is the same.

A DECISION MUST BE MADE

Man must choose whether he will bow his knee to the altar of materialism or drink from the "Fount of Every Blessing." Man must decide whether he will worship at the tabernacle erected by the doctrines and commandments of men, or the church of the living God. But, make no mistake, man cannot serve two masters. Our Lord has said, "No one can serve two masters; for either he will hate the one and love the other, or else he will be loyal to the one and despise the other. You cannot serve God and mammon" (Matthew 6:24). Paul asks us, "Do you not know that to whom you present yourselves slaves to obey, you are that one's slaves whom you obey, whether of sin to death, or of obedience to righteousness?" (Romans 6:16) Peter and the rest of the apostles boldly defended their faith, saying: "We ought to obey God rather than men" (Acts 5:29).

We too must decide whether we will "serve God acceptably with reverence and godly fear" (Hebrews 12:28), or the vain imaginations of an ever-darkening world.

A DECISION MUST BE MADE TODAY

Why do you suppose Joshua wanted the people to make their decision right then and there? I imagine that Joshua felt like God deserved to hear them immediately say that they would choose to serve Him. God deserves to hear us say that today! Just look at all that He has done and will do for us. He will gladly free us from the bondage of sin and has already paid the greatest price possible for our redemption. He deserves to hear us say that we will serve Him *today*!

209

I believe that Joshua also felt like their families needed to know the course their fathers would tread. Joshua was bold enough to let it be known, "But as for me and my house, we will serve the Lord." Our families deserve to know our choice as well. How long must they suffer with our indecision? How many tears must they cry, hoping to persuade us? O' that every man would be the kind of man Joshua was and say, "As for me and my house we shall serve the Lord."

Fathers must become and remain the spiritual leaders of their families. The world needs fathers with a backbone rather than a wishbone! Instead of merely wishing my family was more faithful, as a father, I must set the right example, teach them, and train them to be faithful. "And you, *fathers*, do not provoke your children to wrath, but bring them up in the training and admonition of the Lord" (Ephesians 6:4). I am convinced that fathers like this do not go to heaven alone.

In the third place, I believe Joshua wanted them to be sure that they were committing themselves to a life of service. "And if it seems evil to you to *serve* the Lord, choose for yourselves this day whom you will *serve...*" They answered, "We shall *serve* the Lord." So many people have the attitude that the church is not doing enough to serve them. I cannot help but wonder what they are doing to *serve* the church! As Joshua said, we are to "serve *Him* (not ourselves) in sincerity and in truth."

I'm afraid that many of us approach the faith wondering, "What's it in for me?" Friends, this is not the kind of attitude that will lead to a life of consecrated service. Such an attitude will only lead us down a path of bitter envy and hatred. Let me ask you a candid and personal question: do you seek to have a religious experience or a social exercise? For many, "church" is nothing more than a social exercise. It is

210

something to be done *if* there is nothing better or more pressing to do. For some, "church" is nothing more than a weekly family reunion that allows the grandparents to see the baby! These are the ones who will get mad if the service is too long, or the sermon is too hard, contains too many scriptures, or not enough jokes.

Then there are those who view church as an opportunity to gain stature in the community. For them, "church" is about power, and it provides an opportunity to have a great voice and to flex muscles. These are the ones who cause division and split churches. Guy N. Woods used to say that he would have rather been the soldier who pierced the spear into the Savior's side than to be guilty of causing division in the body of Christ. Do we not realize that the church is the bride of Christ? The church belongs to Christ. He shed His precious blood to purchase the church.

I am worried that many have removed God, His word, and His will from the entire equation. I am worried to see such a lack of willing service on the part of so many "Christians." Do we not realize that we assemble into the very presence of God and we are to worship Him? Have we forgotten that our life is to be a life of consecrated service – a city set on a hill, a light to the world, that men may see our good works and glorify our Father in heaven?

A PERSONAL DECISION

Joshua also wanted to emphasize the fact that this was a personal decision. The people were going to have to make this decision on their own accord.

Some believe you cannot make such a decision, that you are so totally depraved that you cannot choose to serve God. Others believe someone else can make this decision for you by proxy. However, the Bible says, *"Choose you this day."*

Beloved, we have a decision to make that will affect the destiny of our immortal souls. What will be that decision? Will we serve God or self? Will we choose heaven or hell? Where we will spend eternity will be decided by *this* choice we must make for ourselves.

I cannot make your decision for you and you cannot make my decision for me. Only *you* can decide whom *you* will serve and only *I* can decide whom *I* will serve. You can help me to make the right decision just like I can help you. But, ultimately the choice belongs to each one. We each have a personal relationship with God. Let us value this relationship and esteem it above all the other relationships of life.

We each have a choice as to whether or not we will believe that Jesus is the Son of God. Bear in mind that Christ said, "...if you do not believe that I am He, you will die in your sins" (John 8:24).

Each person has a choice this day as to whether or not he will repent of sin or perish in it (Luke 13:3, 5). Repent or perish! The choice is ours to make.

Man can choose this day to confess that Christ is Lord unto salvation, and be baptized to become a child of God by faith (Galatians 3:26-27). You can decide to "arise and be baptized and wash away your sins, calling on the name of the Lord" (Acts 22:16). We can do that. The choice is ours.

The choice is ours as to whether or not we will live faithfully as a Christian. Will we choose to worship faithfully? Will we choose to work faithfully for the Lord? Will we choose to teach others about Him? Choose you this day!

IN CONCLUSION

We have a choice before us, a decision to make. That choice will affect our souls and I believe it will even affect our families and their spiritual outlook. It is a life-altering, destiny-changing choice. Each one must ask himself, "Will I serve the Lord?"

It is also a choice that will be made today. That's right. It *will* be made today. Even if a person decides to do nothing, he has still made a decision. He has decided to do nothing.

Allow me to conclude this lesson by offering one suggestion. Forget you are. Imagine we are in a hospital room, just the two of us. Instead of this being a sermon, it was simply a conversation between two friends. Now, go a little farther and imagine that you are lying there in that hospital bed. I am merely visiting you and discussing such eternally significant matters. I am exhorting you in that hospital room to "choose this day." The doctor knocks at the door and the doctor asks permission to enter. He tells you that your condition is terminal. And, honestly, you know that it is. You have felt your strength slipping away. Death is drawing nigh and you know that you have but a short while remaining in this world.

Having placed yourself into that situation, what would you decide to do with this choice that has been placed before you? *Who* would you choose to obey? *When* do you think you would choose to obey? And, *why* would you choose to obey? Now, if you could give that kind of thoughtful consideration to the well-being of your soul in that dire situation, why can't you do the same now? You might say, "That's different than my situation. I'm not dying." Beloved, we are *all* dying! It is a divine appointment we each must face. God's wonderful mercy and pardon has been extended for dying people to accept!

To choose Him is to accept all that He has done for you. Reject Him, and His amazing grace has been extended in vain – at least as far as your soul is concerned. Choose Him and those scarlet sins shall be washed whiter than snow. Refuse Him, and die without any hope of redemption. Truly the outstretched hand of God reaches for you now. *"Choose for yourselves this day who you will serve."*

THE CLOTHES DON'T MAKE THE MAN

We are blessed to live in a very prosperous country and in a very prosperous time. We live in a land that ever flows with milk and honey. We are all rich people. If you don't believe me, just take a look at the clothes we wear, the cars we drive, and the houses in which we live. It has been stated that if you possess a bank account, some type of housing (regardless of whether you rent or bought your home), and some pocket change of any amount that you are in the top 8% of the wealthiest people in the world.

Seeing that we have been or at least have the opportunity to be very prosperous, we must learn what the Bible says about riches – its responsibilities and its dangers. I see at least three dangers the pursuit of monetary wealth can bring.

In the first place, many people have come to use material things as a measuring rod. They wish to define and classify others by the things they have or do not have – *the haves and have nots.*

The second danger I see is that we can become consumed by an unhealthy zeal for material things. We can become so overly zealous with "stuff" that we become lukewarm in our religion and fail to dedicate ourselves properly in those the things which we ought to be doing. I remember a dear teacher of mine, James Turner, telling us, "The problem with the world today is that people are living for the here and now." He was right on the money with that observation.

My third concern with the pursuit of monetary wealth is taken from Proverbs 11:28: "He who trusts in his riches will fall, But the righteous will flourish like foliage." From this passage we learn that the one who trusts in riches *will* fall – not *may* fall – but *will* fall. It is good to have wealth if we are determined do great things for Christ with it, but if we come to trust in these riches rather than Him, we *will* fall.

Paul's exhorts: "Command those who are rich in this present age not to be haughty, nor to trust in uncertain riches but in the living God, who gives us richly all things to enjoy. Let them do good, that they be rich in good works, ready to give, willing to share, storing up for themselves a good foundation for the time to come, that they may lay hold on eternal life" (1 Timothy 6:17-19).

In order for us to get the full weight of what Paul has said, we should back up a few verses and begin reading from verse six. Read along with me:

"Now godliness with contentment is great gain. (Godliness is not a means of gain (v.5), but to be content in godliness is the great gain.) For we brought nothing into this world, and it is certain we can carry nothing out. And having food and clothing, with these we shall be content. But those who desire to be rich fall into temptation and a snare, and into many foolish and harmful lusts which drown men in destruction and perdition. For the love of money is a root of all kinds of evil, for which some have strayed from the faith in their greediness, and pierced themselves through with many sorrows. But you, O man of God, flee these things and pursue righteousness, godliness, faith, love, patience, gentleness."

Having instructed Timothy accordingly, Paul adds this command: "Command those who are rich in this present age not to be haughty, nor to trust in uncertain riches but in the living God, who gives us richly all things to enjoy. Let them do good, that they be rich in good works, ready to give, willing to share, storing up for themselves a good foundation for the time to come, that they may lay hold on eternal life."

People who "desire to be rich" risk (1) falling into temptation and a snare; (2) being drowned by foolish and harmful lusts; (3) destruction and perdition; (4) all kinds of evil; (5) straying from the faith; (6) being pierced through with many sorrows; (7) becoming haughty; and (8) trusting in these riches rather than God. As Solomon said, "He who trusts in his riches will fall…"

On the other hand, if we live by the truth that "godliness with contentment is great gain," we will (1) be content; (2) flee the lure of the love of money; (3) pursue righteousness, godliness, faith, love, patience, gentleness; (4) trust in the living God; (5) enjoy what we have rather than worrying about what we don't have; (6) do good – even being rich in good works; (7) be ready to give; (8) be willing to share; (9) store up for ourselves a good foundation for the time to come; and (10) lay hold on eternal life. Now, which life do you want to live? Now we can see why Solomon also said, "But the righteous will flourish like foliage."

Undoubtedly, certain things make life a little easier. Many of us have worked hard for what we have. But, we need to keep those things in their proper place. It is a waste of time and life to spend it gathering and coveting material wealth. "Do not overwork to be rich; because of your own understanding, cease! Will you set your eyes on that which is not? For riches certainly make themselves wings; they fly away like an eagle toward heaven" (Proverbs 23:4-5). Again, "For we brought nothing into this world, and it is certain we can carry nothing out" (1 Timothy 6:7).

We must never allow wealth and riches to become our hope or our confidence. Job said, "If I have made gold my hope, Or said to fine gold, 'You are my confidence'; If I have rejoiced because my wealth was so great, And because my hand had gained much; If I have observed the sun when it shines, Or the moon moving in brightness, So that my heart has been secretly enticed, And my mouth has kissed

217

my hand; This also would be an iniquity deserving of judgment, for I would have denied God who is above" (Job 31:24-28).

Brother George Bailey, a great gospel preacher, once said, "Wealth can create a tempest in the harbor, but it cannot establish a harbor in the tempest!" It takes God to do that! We must allow God to rule over our hearts, our minds, and our *bank accounts*!

It is possible to have fine houses, automobiles, and clothes and yet be lost for all eternity. We cannot allow our hearts to be corrupted by these things. Friends, if we are lost on the Judgment Day, all the wealth in the world will not be worth a bale of hay.

A person cannot cover a corrupt heart with fine clothing. In Proverbs 23:7 we read, "for as a man thinks in his heart, so is he." The Lord said, "Blessed are the pure in heart, for they shall see God" (Matthew 5:8). And, "For where your treasure is, there your heart will be also" (Matthew 6:21). The heart – not the clothes – is what makes the man! The heart of man is that which truly defines him in the eyes of God. We must concern ourselves with how our soul is prospering (3 John 2).

THE RICH FOOL

In this lesson, I would like to take three lessons from the Gospel of Luke to illustrate for us that the clothes do not make the man. Let us begin with the parable of the "Rich Fool" (Luke 12:13-21). From this parable, we can clearly see that a person's livelihood can be very prosperous, while the spiritual life is morally bankrupt. Read with me from Luke 12:13-21:

"Then one from the crowd said to Him, 'Teacher, tell my brother to divide the inheritance with me.' But He said to him, 'Man, who made Me a judge or an arbitrator over you?' And He said to them, 'Take heed and beware of covetousness, for one's life does not consist in the abundance of the things he possesses.' Then He spoke a parable to them, saying: 'The ground of a certain rich man yielded plentifully. And he thought within himself, saying, 'What shall I do, since I have no room to store my crops?' So he said, 'I will do this: I will pull down my barns and build greater, and there I will store all my crops and my goods. And I will say to my soul, 'Soul, you have many goods laid up for many years; take your ease; eat, drink, and be merry.' But God said to him, 'You fool! This night your soul will be required of you; then whose will those things be which you have provided?' So is he who lays up treasure for himself, and is not rich toward God.'"

You will observe that this rich farmer had many admirable qualities. He was a hard worker. He earned what he had. He also knew when to retire. I know of many men who simply did not know when to quit. They worked themselves into an early grave. You will also observe that he had a good mind for his business. He made his farm a lucrative business. None of these traits should be taken lightly. Each one speaks to the good qualities of this man. Yet, none of these traits in and of themselves were sufficient to save his soul.

Seeing that a great many qualities can be appreciated about this man, we also realize that his faults were just as obvious. His heart was set only on helping his own cause. He was not rich in good works. He was not ready to give, or willing to share. He was a covetous man and was not rich toward God. He thought his life consisted in the abundance of his possessions. He was a fool in the sight of God. Anyone who pours his soul into material things is a fool in the eyes of God! He spent his life laying up treasures on the earth and failed to lay up any treasure in heaven. The "rich fool" had no spiritual foundation, and did not lay hold of eternal life

Our Lord asked, "Whose will those things be which you have provided?" Again, read with me from Paul's first letter to Timothy: "For we brought nothing into this world, and it is certain we can carry nothing out." When this rich farmer died, he left everything. How much do you suppose he left behind? He left it all. No man can take these uncertain riches beyond the grave. Once we pass through death's door, the only thing that will mean anything to us will be the richness of the relationship we have with God.

THE RICH MAN

If any story illustrates this truth, it is the account of the "rich man" in Luke chapter sixteen. In this chapter, we find a rich man and a poor man named Lazarus. Read with me from Luke 16:19-25:

"There was a certain rich man who was clothed in purple and fine linen and fared sumptuously every day. But there was a certain beggar named Lazarus, full of sores, who was laid at his gate, desiring to be fed with the crumbs which fell from the rich man's table. Moreover the dogs came and licked his sores. So it was that the beggar died, and was carried by the angels to Abraham's bosom. The rich man also died and was buried. And being in torments in Hades, he lifted up his eyes and saw Abraham afar off, and Lazarus in his bosom. Then he cried and said, 'Father Abraham, have mercy on me, and send Lazarus that he may dip the tip of his finger in water and cool my tongue; for I am tormented in this flame.' But Abraham said, 'Son, remember that in your lifetime you received your good things, and likewise Lazarus evil things; but now he is comforted and you are tormented.'"

Herein, Jesus teaches us about a very rich man. I do not know how he attained his great wealth. I only know what he did with it. Judging from his actions we learn that his heart was set only upon "fairing sumptuously every day." He trusted in riches. He was so consumed with sumptuous living that he neglected the poor and needy around him. His religion was not pure and undefiled. He did not live by the "Golden Rule." He did not believe it was more blessed to give than to receive.

He died and was buried. It could be that he paid professional mourners, as was a custom of that day, to give the appearance that a great and beloved man had died. Yet, upon his death, he opened his eyes to see the horror that awaited him. He could also see one of the poor souls he had neglected, Lazarus, seated at the host's table – *Abraham's bosom*. Just imagine what must have gone through his mind.

It is interesting to consider what he said; but it is just as interesting (to me) to consider the things he did not say. Notice, he did not say, "You've got the wrong man! I'm innocent! I don't deserve to be here!" I imagine that upon seeing Lazarus he knew immediately why he was in torment. His world came crashing down as he was reminded of his selfishness and greed and all the people he passed by in his life. He knew why he was there. He was also reminded of his brothers who were obviously living a very similar lifestyle.

He did not make excuses. Rather, he made a request. He asked for a fingertip of water – just a drop of water. He was denied. He asked that Lazarus go and warn his brothers. He was told that his brothers would have to follow God's law and that if they wouldn't listen to the word of

God, they wouldn't listen even though one returned from the dead.

All the money he had in this life could not purchase even a drop of water where he was. All the influence he had in this life could not persuade even one favor being granted in the life beyond. He was now a very poor "rich man." The clothes, the fine linen and purple, could not make the man. His iniquity deserved judgment, for he denied the God who gave him those things. He had been drowned in covetousness unto the point of destruction and perdition. His love of money was a root of all kinds of evil. He was now pierced through with many sorrows.

THE RICH YOUNG RULER

In the case of the rich young ruler, we again learn that the clothes do not make the man. Read with me from Luke 18:18-23:

"Now a certain ruler asked Him, saying, 'Good Teacher, what shall I do to inherit eternal life?' So Jesus said to him, 'Why do you call Me good? No one is good but One, that is, God. You know the commandments: 'Do not commit adultery, 'Do not murder,' 'Do not steal,' 'Do not bear false witness,' 'Honor your father and your mother.' And he said, 'All these I have kept from my youth.' So when Jesus heard these things, He said to him, 'You still lack one thing. Sell all that you have and distribute to the poor, and you will have treasure in heaven; and come, follow Me.' But when he heard this, he became very sorrowful, for he was very rich."

Here we learn of a young man who seemingly had a good rearing and a bright future. I'm sure people admired him for being a good young man. After all, he had kept the Lord's commandments from his youth up. I'm sure his parents must have been very proud of him. The people in his synagogue must have thought highly of him as well. He probably made the people of his hometown very proud. Don't you imagine they doted on this young man all of his life? He obviously was a young man of proven responsibility, for he was titled a "ruler." Indeed, he was a promising figure in his generation.

However, the One who knows the hearts of men said, "You still lack one thing. Sell all that you have and distribute to the poor, and you will have treasure in heaven; and come, follow Me."

The young man went away very sorrowful, for he was very rich. He was as sorrowful as he was rich. He valued his earthly wealth above the treasures of heaven. His greediness caused him to fall. He could not be content, with food and clothing only, he thought he had to have more.

Just consider for a moment, the reality if this young man's opportunity. Here was a man who could have walked with Christ, heard His voice, and spent a portion of his life by the Master's side. What would you give for that chance today? The young man refused a personal invitation from Jesus Christ to be a part of His personal ministry. Why would anyone do such a thing? The answer: *because of money.* Something as trivial as money caused this young man to reject the opportunity countless millions would have given their lives to accept.

Someone will surely say, "Money isn't trivial, preacher! Try living without it!" I ask that you look at this from an eternal perspective. In just a few years, this young man's riches would be meaningless to him. He would die. We are 2,000 years removed from this event. How many times do you suppose the young man has thought of this day and this conversation with our Lord since then? He is living somewhere right now. If he had it to do over again, don't you

223

know he would have given away every dime to be right with Christ? I suppose the answer he gave to Christ on that day has been re-played a trillion times in his mind! We can only hope that he later repented and obeyed the gospel. But, *yes*, from the eternal perspective, money is a very trivial thing!

The young man's sorrowful response prompted the following conversation between the Lord and His disciples: "And when Jesus saw that he became very sorrowful, He said, 'How hard it is for those who have riches to enter the kingdom of God! For it is easier for a camel to go through a needle's eye than for a rich man to enter the kingdom of God.' And those who heard it said, 'Who then can be saved?' But He said, 'The things which are impossible with men are possible with God.' Then Peter said, 'See, we have left all and followed You.' So He said to them, 'Assuredly, I say to you, there is no one who has left house or parents or brothers or wife or children, for the sake of the kingdom of God, who shall not receive *many times more in this present time, and in the age to come everlasting life.*'"

The rich young ruler did not understand the way in which Christ works. Jesus was not asking this of him so that He could hurt him, but to prove him. In fact, Mark says Jesus "beheld him and loved him" in giving His answer (Mark 10:21). Moreover, there was not one thing he would be asked to leave that Christ wasn't able to replace "many times more in this present time, and in the age to come."

In the case of the rich young ruler, the clothes did not make the man. His riches merely proved him to be a worldly-minded, misunderstood, immature man who valued not the true treasures of God. Beloved, the clothes don't make the man.

IN CONCLUSION

We have studied three cases of people who had more dollars than sense. There are people like that today. They spend more time and money on fun and games, clothes and cars, than on the Lord's work and the advancement of the gospel? Beloved, are you defined by your love for God and the love of Christ dwelling in you; or, are you better known for your love of things? In your case, what makes the man?

"Come now, you rich, weep and howl for your miseries that are coming upon you! Your riches are corrupted and your garments are moth-eaten. Your gold and silver are corroded, and their corrosion will be a witness against you and will eat your flesh like fire. You have heaped up treasure in the last days" (James 5:1-3).

Do you have moth-eaten garments stowed away in the attic? Is your wealth rusted and corroded from being hoarded these many years? That rust will be a witness against you on the Judgment Day. Put that money back into circulation. If it's in circulation, it won't rust. Don't trust in rust! Trust in the Lord and use your material blessings to reach the world for Christ, to let your light so shine, and to be an inspiration to others.

Our plea is for all men to give up the carnal passions of worldly materialism and covetousness, and seek those things higher, and pursue those things spiritual, by coming to the cross of Christ. Take it up and bear it henceforth and forevermore. If you are subject to the gospel call in any way, come while your Father longs to bless you, your Savior is waiting to intercede, and mercy lingers still.

THE STORY OF THE BIBLE

In our libraries and book stores of today, there are many books. Solomon wrote, "...of making many books there is no end" (Ecclesiastes 12:12). However, of these many books, there is only *one book* that reveals to us our origin, duty, and destiny. There is only *one book* that can lead us from this earthly life to a heavenly home.

You will find that this book is titled, "Holy Bible." The Bible begins by directing man to God. "In the beginning God created the heavens and the earth" (Genesis 1:1). It is comprised of sixty-six individual books – thirty-nine in the Old Testament and twenty-seven being in the New Testament. The Bible was written by at least forty devout men over a period of approximately twenty-five hundred years. It was revealed "at various times and in different ways" (Hebrews 1:1). It is the very word of God, containing at least two thousand times the phrase, "Thus says the Lord," or the equivalent thereof. Through His word, God offers us necessary encouragement, correction, and comfort for our lives.

THE PATRIARCHAL AGE

The Bible tells of the three ages of human history – the Patriarchal, Mosaic, and Christian Age. The Patriarchal Age lasted some twenty-five hundred years. During this age of history events happened such as mankind's beginning. Make no mistake, man is a created being. "Then God said, 'Let Us make man in Our image, according to Our likeness; let them have dominion over the fish of the sea, over the birds of the air, and over the cattle, over all the earth and over every creeping thing that creeps on the earth'" (Genesis 1:26). "And the Lord God formed man of the dust of the ground, and breathed into his nostrils the breath of life; and man became a living being" (Genesis 2:7).

Woman is also a created being, although she was created a little differently. "And the Lord God said, 'It is not good that man should be alone; I will make him a helper comparable to him'" (Genesis 2:18). Isn't it amazing to consider that God was pleased with everything He had made with one exception – "it is not good that man should be alone." "And the Lord God caused a deep sleep to fall on Adam, and he slept; and He took one of his ribs, and closed up the flesh in its place. Then the rib which the Lord God had taken from man He made into a woman, and He brought her to the man" (Genesis 2:21-22).

Adam understood perfectly the sacred bond of this union. He would speak the following by divine revelation, "This is now bone of my bones and flesh of my flesh; she shall be called Woman, because she was taken out of Man. Therefore a man shall leave his father and mother and be joined to his wife, and they shall become one flesh" (Genesis 2:23-24).

It was during the Patriarchal Age that father Adam experienced his fall. In Genesis chapter three the deceiver and adversary is introduced. Satan changed only one word in God's divine revelation to lead Eve astray. He said, "Thou shalt *not* surely die." He also changed her perception of the righteousness of God, falsely accusing that God, "knows that in the day you eat of it your eyes will be opened, and you will be like God, knowing good and evil." Eve then gave to Adam and he did also eat from the tree.

After they had attempted to cover themselves and hide from the presence of God, He asked them simply, "Where are you?" I believe that is a question worth asking today. It was not that God did not know, but God wanted *them* to know.

Two profound truths can be learned about the nature of sin from the fall in Eden. First, our sins hurt God. Our sins grieve and can even anger God. And secondly, our sins cannot be hidden from God. "And there is no creature hidden from His sight, but all things are naked and open to the eyes of Him to whom we must give account" (Hebrews 4:13).

From the fall in the garden we also learn of mankind's hope. From the seed of woman a crushing death blow would be struck to the head of Satan (Genesis 3:15). God said from the seed of woman the death blow would come. He was speaking of Jesus who was born of a virgin, begotten of the Holy Spirit.

God would extend a promise to Abraham, Isaac, and Jacob that would be from that family that "all the families of the earth shall be blessed" (Genesis 12:3). Again, He was speaking of Christ. Jesus came from the seed of Abraham. He is the Lion of the tribe of Judah, the Root of Jesse, and Son of David. How would this promise be fulfilled? How would God make of one seed every nation, kindred, people, and tongue? This great mystery leads us into the Mosaic Age.

THE MOSAIC AGE

The Mosaic Age lasted approximately fifteen hundred years. A great famine had caused Abraham's seed, the children Israel, to seek refuge in Egypt. Joseph, a son of Israel, became the right hand of Pharaoh. Seventy souls of the house of Israel went down into Egypt and "were fruitful and increased abundantly, multiplied and grew exceedingly mighty; and the land was filled with them" (Exodus 1:7).

229

But, there arose a king in Egypt who knew not Joseph and enslaved Israel for an estimated one hundred and forty years.

God would choose two brothers to lead Israel out of Egypt – Moses and Aaron. When God first came to Moses, Moses offered nothing but excuses as to why he was not the man for the job. One of the great stories to be found in Exodus through Deuteronomy is the maturation of Moses. He was not a great leader when God found him, but he *became* a great leader.

God would send these two brothers unto Pharaoh with the demand, "Let my people go." Pharaoh hardened his heart against God, bringing a total of ten plagues upon himself and his people. After all of this, Pharaoh was so hardened and bitter that he reneged on his word and pursued the Israelites who were leaving. Here was a man that had seen firsthand the power of God and, moreover, would come to the brink of the Red Sea to find the waters parted and the bottom dried. Knowing Israel had already passed safely to the other side, Pharaoh drove his army into the midst of those congealed waters to meet their swift and sudden destruction. Now what would make a man act so foolishly, but pride? He could not let God have the final word and it cost him his life and his soul.

After only a few days in the Wilderness, the Jews began murmuring and complaining against Moses and God. After all that God had done for them, they accused Him of bringing them into the wilderness to die!

While they were in the Wilderness, the Law of Moses was given to Israel at Mount Sinai (Galatians 3:19). The Law was added to serve as a schoolmaster for Israel to bring them unto the faith of Christ (Galatians 3:24). It was added temporarily until the giving of the "new covenant" (Jeremiah 31:31). The Law was fulfilled completely by Christ and

230

when He nailed to His cross (Colossians 2:14). No man has the right to judge any man by that law anymore (Colossians 2:16).

Moses would not be allowed to enter the Promised Land because he disobeyed God and struck the rock twice, rather than speaking to it. His mantle fell upon Joshua. Joshua led the conquest of Canaan. He was followed by a succession of Judges. During this period, Israel was continually given to idolatry. They would fall away from the Lord, become oppressed by their enemies, repent and cry out for deliverance and God would raise a judge or deliverer to save them.

One would think that Israel would have learned after the first time they were oppressed by their enemies, maybe the second. But the heart of the people had waxed gross due to the influences of the idolatrous people they had taken for wives and the evil influence that existed in that land. They would not have had this problem had they obeyed God and utterly destroyed the inhabitants of the land; but they did not. Judges closes by saying, "In those days there was no king in Israel; everyone did what was right in his own eyes." How sad indeed.

The last of the Judges was a prophet named Samuel. He took it personally when the people said, "Look, you are old, and your sons do not walk in your ways. Now make for us a king to judge us like all the nations" (1 Samuel 8:5). But God knew the true intent of the people, and instructed Samuel thusly: "Heed the voice of the people in all that they say to you; for they have not rejected you, but they have rejected Me, that I should not reign over them."

Samuel would anoint a man from the tribe of Benjamin, named Saul, as the first King of Israel. Saul was a great warrior-king. Yet, he presumed he knew the mind of God better than God. On one occasion, Saul decided to offer a burnt offering which he had no authority to offer. Instead of patiently waiting for Samuel, he took it upon himself. Samuel rebuked this act by saying, "You have done foolishly. You have not kept the commandment of the Lord your God, which He commanded you. For now the Lord would have established your kingdom over Israel forever. But now your kingdom shall not continue. The Lord has sought for Himself a man after His own heart, and the Lord has commanded him to be commander over His people, because you have not kept what the Lord commanded you" (1 Samuel 13:13-14).

Anytime we do something religiously that God has not authorized, we are doing foolishly. On the second occasion of presumptuous sin, King Saul was commanded thusly: "Now go and attack Amalek, and utterly destroy all that they have, and do not spare them. But kill both man and woman, infant and nursing child, ox and sheep, camel and donkey" (1 Samuel 15:3). Rather than doing this, Saul thought it was better to spare "Agag and the best of the sheep, the oxen, the fatlings, the lambs, and all that was good, and were unwilling to utterly destroy them (He said that he did this in order to make a sacrifice to God (v.15). But everything despised and worthless, that they utterly destroyed" (v.9).

Therefore, God said to Samuel, "I greatly regret that I have set up Saul as king, for he has turned back from following Me, and has not performed My commandments" (v.11). And upon visiting King Saul, Samuel rebuked him again by saying: "Now the Lord sent you on a mission, and said, 'Go, and utterly destroy the sinners, the Amalekites, and fight against them until they are consumed.' Why then did you not obey the voice of the Lord? Why did you swoop down on the spoil, and do evil in the sight of the Lord? ... Has the Lord as great delight in burnt offerings and sacrifices, as in obeying the voice of the Lord? Behold, to obey is better than sacrifice, and to heed than the fat of rams. For rebellion is as the sin of witchcraft, and stubbornness is as iniquity and idolatry. Because you have rejected the word of the Lord, He also has rejected you from being king" (vv. 18-19; 22-23).

In 1 Samuel chapter sixteen, Samuel would anoint young David as Saul's successor. David would reign for forty years and be succeeded by his son Solomon. Solomon would also reign for forty years and give us such books and Proverbs, Ecclesiastes, and Song of Solomon.

Upon Solomon's death, Israel would be divided into two kingdoms. Rehoboam, the son of Solomon would reign over the tribes of Judah and Benjamin in what was called the Southern Kingdom of Judah. Jeroboam the son of Nebat would reign over the ten remaining tribes of the Northern Kingdom of Israel. The righteous from all the tribes, many being from the tribe of Simeon, and the Levites gathered with Judah (2 Chronicles 11:13-17).

The Northern Kingdom of Israel was vexed by wicked leadership and idolatry from the beginning of their existence. This kingdom had nineteen kings and every last one of them was wicked to the core. They were subjugated to Assyrian captivity in 722 BC, and never returned to their homeland.

One would think that the fate befalling their brethren to the north would have been a reasonable cause for the Kingdom of Judah to remain on a straight and narrow path. However, they would stubbornly suffer the same fate. Jeremiah provides a great insight to their rebellious ways. The Southern Kingdom would fall to the Babylonians, finally being carried captive in 586 BC. However, God would allow a remnant to return and re-establish themselves in their homeland. He did this knowing that it would be through these people that His Son would come into the world.

Persia would go on to defeat Babylon and the Persian King Cyrus would allow his captain Zerubbabel to lead 50,000 Jews back to Palestine with the first of three such groups (535 BC). The Temple was dedicated again in 516 BC. Ezra preached and led his reforms around 458 BC. Nehemiah would rebuild the city walls of Jerusalem and continue with his religious reforms (445 BC). The Books of Daniel, Esther, Ezra, and Nehemiah are especially critical to understanding this period.

Four hundred silent years would follow the reforms of Ezra and Nehemiah. During these years there was no divine revelation given to Israel. Groups like the Pharisees and Sadducees became prominent among the Jews. Three separate kingdoms would come to succeed each other in ruling the world. They are in order: the Medo-Persian Empire, Alexander the Great and his Greek Empire, and finally Caesar's Roman Empire. Each of which was prophesied by Daniel to the Babylonian King Nebuchadnezzar during the interpretation of a dream (Daniel 2). The evil Herodian Dynasty would also become the rulers in Palestine.

It was during the time of Roman rule throughout the world and Herodian rule in Palestine that the Babe of Bethlehem was born (3-5 BC). In Christ, the mystery of the Old Testament is revealed. "And without controversy great is the mystery of godliness: God was manifested in the flesh, justified in the Spirit, seen by angels, preached among the Gentiles, believed on in the world, received up in glory" (1 Timothy 3:16). In Christ, the Law of Moses is fulfilled (Matthew 5:17-18; Colossians 2:14). In Christ, man is reconciled to God so completely by the cross (Ephesians 2:16), so that our sins might be remembered no more (Hebrews 10:17).

His death took away the first covenant, the Old Law, so that He might establish the second covenant (Hebrews 10:9). The final age of human history was inaugurated, which is the Christian Age.

THE CHRISTIAN AGE

The Christian Age is "the dispensation of the fullness of times" (Ephesians 1:10). This is the age in which we are now living. It is the greatest age ever known to man. It has been said that the age of the Patriarchs was the "starlight" age; the age of the Law was the "moonlight" age; but the age of Christ is the "sunlight" age – the brightest age of all!

The Christian dispensation began when Christ purchased His church and inaugurated His gospel by His death on the cross (Hebrews 9:15). Throughout the Christian Age, sinners must obey the gospel of Jesus Christ to be saved. Christians must live by the gospel as the law which is governing His kingdom.

By His death, Jesus established His kingdom. His kingdom is His church (Matthew 16:18-19). God adds us to this kingdom when we obey the gospel (2 Thessalonians 2:14). "He has delivered us from the power of darkness and translated us into the kingdom of the Son of His love, in whom we have redemption through His blood, the forgiveness of sins" (Colossians 1:13-14). It is a kingdom that shall stand forever. "Therefore, since we are receiving a kingdom which cannot be shaken, let us have grace, by which we may serve God acceptably with reverence and godly fear" (Hebrews 10:28).

The Bible also teaches us about the success that this kingdom can have. The early Christians were powerful people! They took the gospel throughout the world (Colossians 1:6). They were not ashamed of what they believed or who they served. They faced persecutions from within and without. These brethren had many opportunities to quit. Yet, they persevered and the gospel spread like a prairie fire across the ancient world.

The Christian Age will continue until the Lord returns and the final Judgment takes place. No man knows when this day will come. "But of that day and hour no one knows, no, not even the angels of heaven, but My Father only" (Matthew 24:36). "But the day of the Lord will come as a thief in the night, in which the heavens will pass away with a great noise, and the elements will melt with fervent heat; both the earth and the works that are in it will be burned up" (2 Peter 3:10). He is coming a "second time" (Hebrews 9:28), or "once more" (Hebrews 12:26).

At His return, Christians will be raised to meet the Lord in the air (2 Thessalonians 4:16-18), the earth will be destroyed (2 Peter 3:10-13), all mankind will be judged (Matthew 25:31-46), the unrighteous will be cast into eternal hell (Revelation 20:14-15), and the righteous will go into life eternal (Revelation 21:1-7). Are *you* ready for the day of the Lord?

IN CONCLUSION

The Bible is God's revelation of His nature, His dealings with man, and His plan to save us. One might say simply that Jesus Christ is the story of the Bible. He is that golden thread of divine revelation that connects Genesis to Revelation. If not for Jesus, there would be no Bible.

The story of the Bible is the greatest story ever told. Our hearts are inspired by reading it. Our emotions are uplifted by believing it. Our souls are saved by obeying it. "And the

Spirit and the bride say, 'Come!' And let him who hears say, 'Come!' And let him who thirsts come. And whoever desires, let him take the water of life freely" (Revelation 22:17).

"He who testifies to these things says, 'Surely I am coming quickly.' Amen. Even so, come, Lord Jesus! The grace of our Lord Jesus Christ be with you all. Amen" (Revelation 22:20-21).

DOES THE CHURCH NEED A REVIVAL?

Does the church need a revival? First, let me state that "revival" in the sense in which we are using it means, "a restoration to vigor or activity." The Christian religion is a pro-active religion. God's word must be put into action. When we stop at hearing and do not put the word into action we deceive ourselves (James 1:22). His word is the seed of the kingdom (Luke 8:11). For any seed to be effective it must be planted – it must be put into action. As long as the seed sits on the shelf, it is dormant. But, when it is planted, it takes root and bears fruit.

God promises that His word will work if it is planted. It will not return to Him without accomplishing its purpose (Isaiah 55:10-11). God will provide the increase if the seed is sown and watered (1 Corinthians 3:6-8).

DOES THE WORK OF THE CHURCH NEED A REVIVAL?

The future of the church depends upon Christians being "doers of the word." Consider the example of the Jerusalem congregation. They filled Jerusalem with their doctrine (Acts 5:28). As a result, many thousands came to believe (Acts 21:20). Also consider the example of the church in Thessalonica. These brethren understood the need to have a "work of faith, labor of love, and patience of hope" (1 Thessalonians 1:3). Paul said of them, "Your faith toward God has gone out, so that we do not need to say anything" (1 Thessalonians 1:8).

The need for revival can be properly illustrated by the children of Israel. God brought them out of bondage, supplied their every need, and provided great promises to sustain their spirits. "Yet they did not obey or incline their ear, but walked in the counsels and in the imagination of their evil heart, and went backward and not forward. Since the day that your fathers came out of the land of Egypt until this day, I have even sent to you all My servants the prophets, daily rising up early and sending them. Yet they did not obey Me or incline their ear, but stiffened their neck. They did worse than their fathers." (Jeremiah 7:24-26).

Is this not an accurate depiction of digression? Because of such rebellion, the children of Israel were in constant need of revival. David pleaded with God, "Restore us, O God of our salvation, And cause Your anger toward us to cease. Will You be angry with us forever? Will You prolong Your anger to all generations? Will You not revive us again, That Your people may rejoice in You?" (Psalm 85:4-6)

In order for a revival to occur, a restoration must take place. "For thus says the High and Lofty One Who inhabits eternity, whose name is Holy: 'I dwell in the high and holy place, with him who has a contrite and humble spirit, to revive the spirit of the humble, and to revive the heart of the contrite ones'" (Isaiah 57:15).

The need for revival is also illustrated in five of the seven churches of Asia. In Revelation chapters two and three we find examples of such churches of Christ as Ephesus who left their first love, Pergamos and Thyatira who had false teachers in their midst, Sardis which was alive in name only, and Laodicea which was lukewarm in their religion.

Philadelphia and Smyrna were the only congregations the Lord commended. Have you ever noticed that some communities and even churches are named after Philadelphia and Smyrna? But, have you ever found one named after any of these others? Does this not suggest to you that no one wants to honor a church that does not "do the word" and put the truth and their religion into practice?

In each of these cases, we see the need for revival. Repentance was their only cure. Again, we learn that for a revival to occur, repentance and restoration must take place.

You will also observe that in each instance, the Lord could point to certain indicators which spoke of the need for revival. For Ephesus, they had lost the zeal that once characterized their congregation. For Pergamos, they were allowing such sins as fornication to continue, while false teachers only helped to promote and foster such wickedness. In Thyatira you will find a congregation suffering a "Jezebel" type of woman to teach and seduce the brethren to err. Sardis was a congregation trying to make it on past achievements and former faithfulness. They had a name that carried great weight in the brotherhood, but the Lord knew their faith was dead. Laodicea was a church satisfied with going through the motions. They had lost their zeal. They had lost their desire to *go* and *grow* for the Lord. They were strictly going through the motions, and "keeping the doors open."

Today, I believe we can also tell by similar indications whether or not we are in need of revival. Such indicators may be a lack of Bible study, negligent worship attendance, or even compromising what we know to be true and right. I am convinced that when this need for revival goes unmet, apostasy and death will be the eventual fate of any congregation.

More often than not, a gradual slackness in meeting the responsibilities the Lord has given us will precede the obvious result of outright waywardness. Worship attendance gradually declines on the part of some. In some congregations, the Bible is gradually studied less and less. When new doctrines and doubts are introduced a little at a time, apostasy is inevitable. The church may even decide to table many

241

good works they once strongly performed, rather than finding a way to keep them going.

Beloved, the church must maintain its good works to succeed. "For God is not unjust to forget your work and labor of love which you have shown toward His name, in that you have ministered to the saints, and do minister. And we desire that each one of you show the same diligence to the full assurance of hope until the end, that you do not become sluggish, but imitate those who through faith and patience inherit the promises. (Hebrews 6:10-12).

Any congregation not committed to growing stronger is at risk of becoming weaker. If we are not committed to growing stronger, we will become more susceptible to false doctrine. We'll be prone to complacency, and we will see our brothers and sisters becoming more apt to fall away in times of temptation.

The salvation of precious souls depends upon our doing the word. The souls in this community and in our families are precious. Just consider the price God paid to redeem them. Consider the great conflict being waged over them. Also consider the great regard Christ holds for them. Our own soul is also precious to God. As Christians, we must keep learning, growing, and following Christ.

The crown jewel of 1 Corinthians is found in chapter fifteen and verse fifty-eight: "Therefore, my beloved brethren, be steadfast, immovable, always abounding in the work of the Lord, knowing that your labor is not in vain in the Lord" (1 Corinthians 15:58).

We must have this attitude. Paul could honestly say, "For I am already being poured out as a drink offering, and the time of my departure is at hand. I have fought the good fight, I have finished the race, I have kept the faith. Finally, there is laid up for me the crown of righteousness, which the

Lord, the righteous Judge, will give to me on that Day, and not to me only but also to all who have loved His appearing" (2 Timothy 4:6-8).

DOES THE ATTITUDE OF THE CHURCH NEED A REVIVAL?

Please tell me, do think God is happy with us when we do not take our religion seriously? Do you think God is happy with us when we murmur, backbite, and stir wrath and strife among our brethren? Who is glorified when we gripe and complain about the church? Do you think God wants that nonsense in heaven? Who is given the glory when we allow murmuring and complaining to rule the church? Have you ever known of a congregation that became better by yielding to unfaithful "yelpers?"

I'll tell you plainly, beloved, if you want to kill your home congregation, just yield to the unfaithful, backbiting, do-nothing complainers and you will surely destroy it. The Lord said He would bring His judgment upon those unfaithful congregations of Asia and He did just that. God will do the same today when necessary. I believe many of you know that to be true.

Do you think a godly-minded person in this or any community would want to be in spiritual fellowship with a person who was a gossip, a drunkard, an adulterer, a liar, a cheat, or a rabble-rouser? Do you think such people look at Christians who live that way and desire to be like them? God said, "Be ye holy for I am holy." Christ said, "Let your light so shine before men that they may see your good works and glorify your Father in heaven."

Who do we glorify when we leave our first love? Who is glorified when false doctrine is taught? Who is given the glory when we boast of sin by the lives we live?

243

Some Christians are outspoken in their refusal to repent of their cherished sins. Even though they live in sin, stubborn pride, and refuse to repent, congregations continue to permit them to serve the Lord's Table, lead prayers, and even teach in Bible classes. My brethren, "these things ought not to be."

Who is given the glory when we stake our souls on things we *used* to do? You give me a congregation that talks about all the work they *used* to do and I'll show you a congregation missing the people that *used* to attend and all the baptisms they *used* to have.

Who is given the glory when we become lukewarm in our religion? Does a lukewarm religion bring any glory to God? Does this kind of religion any heart with joy? Does this kind of religion bring any hope or happiness? Loved ones, if you are a Christian, and have no joy, hope, or happiness in your faith, your faith needs a revival! We need to have Isaiah's attitude when it comes to the work of the church. "Here am I send me" (Isaiah 6:8). When is the last time you said that to your elders? When is the last time you said that about teaching, helping, and working in the Lord's church?

DOES THE VOICE OF THE CHURCH NEED A REVIVAL?

Brethren, we have a great evil among us. This great evil is the evil of "do-nothing-ism." Who is given the glory when we allow nay-saying to quiet the gospel? Who is glorified when the Lord's truth cannot be taught and is silenced? Who is glorified when faithful gospel preachers are fired for preaching and standing for the truth? Who is glorified when liberalism takes over a once faithful congregation like a suffocating kudzu vine?

244

Brethren, the Lord is calling upon us to wake up. "Therefore He says: 'Awake, you who sleep, arise from the dead, and Christ will give you light'" (Ephesians 5:14).

"Therefore let us not sleep, as others do, but let us watch and be sober. For those who sleep, sleep at night, and those who get drunk are drunk at night. But let us who are of the day be sober, putting on the breastplate of faith and love, and as a helmet the hope of salvation" (1 Thessalonians 5:6-8).

"Do not be deceived: 'Evil company corrupts good habits.' Awake to righteousness, and do not sin; for some do not have the knowledge of God. I speak this to your shame" (1 Corinthians 15:33-34).

The Lord is going to judge His people and every person that offends will be cast into outer darkness. "For we know Him who said, 'Vengeance is Mine; I will repay, says the Lord.' And again, "The Lord will judge His people. It is a fearful thing to fall into the hands of the living God" (Hebrews 10:30-31).

Our brethren who do err from the truth may think they are getting away with something by dominating their brethren with satanic agendas, but the all-seeing eye of God is watching every step they take. They are going to pay for the hurt and shame they have brought upon the church. The Lord says, "And behold, I am coming quickly, and My reward is with Me, to give to every one according to his work" (Revelation 22:12).

Sin is evident in brethren who cause division in the Lord's church. Sin is furthermore evident in those who do not care. Paul said, "Now I urge you, brethren, note those who cause divisions and offenses, contrary to the doctrine which you learned, and avoid them" (Romans 16:17).

John said, "Whoever transgresses and does not abide in the doctrine of Christ does not have God. He who abides in the doctrine of Christ has both the Father and the Son. If anyone comes to you and does not bring this doctrine, do not receive him into your house nor greet him; for he who greets him shares in his evil deeds" (2 John 9-11).

Paul writes, "But we command you, brethren, in the name of our Lord Jesus Christ, that you withdraw from every brother who walks disorderly and not according to the tradition which he received from us" (2 Thessalonians 3:6).

The need for revival is evident when sin takes over. Sin is a transgression of God's law (1 John 3:4). Sin can occur when we go beyond the word of God or when we take from the word of God. We can sin by committing unholy deeds or by failing to do what God has commanded. All unrighteousness is sin (1 John 5:17). Whatever religious act or doctrine not done out of faith is sin (Romans 14:23).

The bottom line is simply, *sin is sin.* Regardless of how you try to explain it, justify it, or soften it. Sin is sin. Sin is unholy. Sin will cost us our souls. "The wages of sin is death" (Romans 6:23). Sin brings forth death (James 1:15). Sin will ruin our lives on earth and the life we hope to spend in eternity.

IN CONCLUSION

We speak of the need for revival so that we might take sin seriously. When asked what he thought was the greatest need facing the church, V.P. Black said, "I don't know what all is wrong, but I know basically what is wrong. We have far too many members attempting to serve God who have never been crucified to the world. We need a great crucifixion in the church."

Paul said of himself, "I have been crucified with Christ; it is no longer I who live, but Christ lives in me; and the life which I now live in the flesh I live by faith in the Son of God, who loved me and gave Himself for me" (Galatians 2:20). Furthermore, he said, "But God forbid that I should glory except in the cross of our Lord Jesus Christ, by whom the world has been crucified to me, and I to the world" (Galatians 6:14).

Can you say this of yourself? Does this not explain why Paul was able to do all that he did for Christ? His religion was a true, sacrificial faith in Christ. In giving himself to Christ, he died to the world. He understood that he could not serve two masters.

Allow me to conclude by urging you to have a deep, devotional faith in Christ. Give Him your life. Love Him with all you heart, soul, mind, and strength. Realize that all you ever hope to be is in Him. Empty yourself before God and hold nothing back. If you are in need of a spiritual revival, Jesus is the answer. He is the only answer. If you will come to Christ, a great revival can occur in your life.

FROM THE HEART AND FROM THE BIBLE

The Scriptures are filled with accounts of men and women both obeying and disobeying God. In every instance of obedience, we will find a person obeying God from his heart and from God's word. In every instance of disobedience, we find a person doing *other than*, *more than*, or *less than* what God has commanded. Sometimes their hearts were sincere and sometimes they were not.

ACCOUNTS OF DISOBEDIENCE—OTHER THAN

In the case of Nadab and Abihu, we find an example of two brothers doing *other than* what the Lord commanded. In Leviticus 10:1, we read that these two brothers, sons of Aaron, offered strange or profane fire before the Lord, "which He had not commanded them." In verse two, we learn that fire went out from the Lord and devoured them. We cannot establish their motives for certain, but we know for certain that they did not do as God commanded.

A few years later, the Lord commanded Joshua, "Only be strong and very courageous, that you may observe to do according to all the law which Moses My servant commanded you; do not turn from it to the right hand or to the left, that you may prosper wherever you go" (Joshua 1:7).

Apparently, Achan thought this principle did not apply to him. In Joshua chapter seven, we read of Israel's stunning defeat at Ai because Achan had brought sin into the camp. Israel would not prevail as long as the "accursed thing" was among them. What did Achan do that was so wrong? He did *other than* what God commanded. God told them not to take of Jericho's spoils. Achan thought, "What's wrong with just a few things?" When confronted, he confessed, "When I saw among the spoils a beautiful Babylonian garment, two hundred shekels of silver, and a wedge of gold weighing fifty shekels, I coveted them and took them" (Joshua 7:21). Joshua said, "Why have you troubled us? The Lord will trouble you this day."

Trouble did come for Achan as, "all Israel stoned him with stones; and they burned them with fire after they had stoned them with stones. Then they raised over him a great heap of stones, still there to this day. So the Lord turned from the fierceness of His anger. Therefore the name of that place has been called the Valley of Achor to this day" (Joshua 7:25-26).

A similar occasion is found in 1 Samuel chapter fifteen. Herein we find Saul doing other than the Lord commanded. Samuel said to Saul, "The Lord sent me to anoint you king over His people, over Israel. Now therefore, heed the voice of the words of the Lord. Thus says the Lord of hosts: 'I will punish what Amalek did to Israel, how he laid wait for him on the way when he came up from Egypt. Now go and attack Amalek, and utterly destroy all that they have, and do not spare them. But kill both man and woman, infant and nursing child, ox and sheep, camel and donkey'" (1 Samuel 15:1-3).

Saul did attack the Amalekites, "from Havilah all the way to Shur, which is east of Egypt. He also took Agag king of the Amalekites alive, and utterly destroyed all the people with the edge of the sword. But Saul and the people spared Agag and the best of the sheep, the oxen, the fatlings, the lambs, and all that was good, and were unwilling to utterly destroy them. But everything despised and worthless, that they utterly destroyed" (1 Samuel 15:7-9).

Saul may have thought he was making a wise decision, but truthfully he was guilty of not obeying the Lord. The Lord told Samuel, "I greatly regret that I have set up Saul as king, for he has turned back from following Me, and has not performed My commandments" (1 Samuel 15:11).

Saul thought he could bring these things back and offer them as a sacrifice to the Lord. Samuel asked him, "Why then did you not obey the voice of the Lord? Why did you swoop down on the spoil, and do evil in the sight of the Lord?" (1 Samuel 15:19)

Samuel continued, "Has the Lord as great delight in burnt offerings and sacrifices, as in obeying the voice of the Lord? Behold, to obey is better than sacrifice, and to heed than the fat of rams" (1 Samuel 15:22). From that day onward, Saul was rejected as king. Disobedience to God will only bring displeasure and rejection.

In the case of David, Uzzah, and the Ark of the Covenant, we learn of someone doing other than what the Lord commanded (2 Samuel 6:3-7). David thought it was better to place the Ark upon "a new cart," rather than having the priests carry it with staves upon their shoulders as God commanded. The Ark began to rattle and looked as though it was about to fall when Uzzah rushed to brace it. The moment he touched it he fell dead. Uzzah was sincere. He honestly thought he was doing the right thing. But, God commanded that the Ark be carried with staves upon four priests' shoulders and said that it was not to be touched. That command included Uzzah. Even though David and Uzzah had good intentions, they were guilty of doing something other than God commanded and it cost Uzzah his life.

Now let's talk about doing *other than* what God has commanded as it applies for today. The Bible says we should be baptized to wash our sins away (Acts 22:16). Yet, men say you can offer a "sinner's prayer." Where is this prayer commanded by God? Where is this prayer in the Scriptures? God commands us to be baptized (Mark 16:16;

251

Acts 2:38). Where does God command sinners to pray for salvation?

The Bible teaches us about the church. The Bible does not teach us to join or be voted into denominations. To belong to a denomination is to do something other than what God has commanded. In these denominations, you find women preachers, pastoral systems, creeds, catechisms, and such like. Not one of these ideas is Scriptural. In fact, the Scriptures command exactly the opposite of these practices.

A person does not have to do these unscriptural things. No one has to belong to a church, take part in a practice, or endorse a doctrine not in God's word. It is quite the opposite, actually. Everyone can belong to the same church as did Peter and Paul. Each person can worship God just as they did. All can obey God by doing as they did. Friends, no one has to do a single thing not commanded by God. God is not requiring for anyone to do or be anything more than, other than, or less than what He has commanded.

ACCOUNTS OF DISOBEDIENCE—MORE THAN

When we come into New Testament times, we find cases of similar disobedience as are found in the Old Testament. In the case of the Pharisees and the tradition of washing hands (Matthew 15), we find an example of people doing *more than* the Lord commanded. Mind you, there is nothing wrong with washing your hands. I'm told that this practice helps to prevent sickness and common colds. However, the Pharisees sinned because they made washing hands a religious rite which God never commanded. They were *adding* to the word of God.

Concerning circumcision, nothing is wrong with having a child circumcised, as long as we do not make it a religious rite of passage. Paul said that neither circumcision nor un-circumcision avails for anything (Galatians 5:6).

Nothing is wrong with a great many things we do every day, but that does not give us the right to make a religious practice out of them. A modern day application of *doing more* than God has commanded is the use of instrumental music in worship. God commands us to sing (Ephesians 5:19; Colossians 3:16). God has commanded this type of music to be conducted in the church. God has not command-ed the church to conduct music through the use of mechani-cal instruments. Nothing is wrong with playing or listening to these instruments as a hobby or for pleasure. But, when it comes to having these things in a religious service, and mak-ing a religious practice out of them, we must have God's commandment to authorize the act. If He has not authorized the act, we do not have the right to introduce it.

The same is true with washing infants. Anyone who has ever cared for an infant has bathed that baby. It is certainly not sinful to pour water on a baby's head to wash out any shampoo. But, if I were to make something religious out of it and say that they must have water poured on their head as a religious rite in order to be saved, I would be guilty of do-ing more than God has commanded. We have people pour-ing water onto little children every day in certain denomina-tional churches. They have no biblical grounds for the act, but they do it regardless. They have made a law God never made. They have added to His word.

I do not know of anything wrong with burning candles or incense in my home. But, I have no right to make this a re-ligious practice which God never commanded. When we do more than, less than, or other than what God has command-ed, our actions will be more than, less than, or other than those of a soul-saving faith. The great preacher M.C. Kurfees understood, "It is still true that whenever and wherever men do, as religious service, what they are not commanded to do, it is rejected."

ACCOUNTS OF DISOBEDIENCE—LESS THAN

In the case of the Jews of Paul's day, we have an example of souls doing *less than* God's commandments regarding His Son. They refused to accept Christ. They refused to obey His gospel. They did not accept His word. They rejected His kingdom. They had "zeal for God, but not according to knowledge. For being ignorant of God's righteousness, and seeking to establish their own righteousness, they have not submitted to the righteousness of God" (Romans 10:2-3).

They had religious zeal, but they were zealously mistaken. Zeal is not enough. Man must have zeal *and* knowledge. Because of their lack of knowledge and refusal to obey the word of God, they sought to establish their own righteousness. Such is the case today whenever men think they can usurp God's commandments and establish their own religion.

A modern day application of this attitude of doing *less than* God commands is seen in forsaking the assembly of the church. The Bible says we are not to forsake "the assembling of ourselves together, as the manner of some is, but encourage one another, and so much the more as you see the day approaching" (Hebrews 10:25). Yet, someone will say, "You don't have to go to church." They are content to do *less than* the Lord has commanded.

Others will say they do not need to partake of the Lord's Supper every time they are assembled on the Lord's Day. However, the Bible says this is one of the primary reasons we are to come together (1 Corinthians 11:17 ff.).

Another example of this type of disobedience is found in rejecting baptism. Some will say, "You do not have to be baptized." The Lord said, "Except a man is born of water and Spirit, he shall not enter the kingdom of God" (John 3:5). The Lord said, "He that believes and is baptized shall be saved..." (Mark 16:16).

ACCOUNTS OF OBEDIENCE—FROM THE HEART AND FROM THE BIBLE

For man's religion to be pleasing to God, it must be from the heart and from the Bible. It cannot be from the heart only and it cannot be from the Bible only. If it is a "heart only" religion, it will not be founded on the Scriptures. If it is a "Bible only" religion, it will be cold, ritualistic, and insincere.

We must be sincere in our religion. However, a person can be sincere and yet sincerely wrong. One such case of a person being sincerely mistaken is the young prophet of 1 Kings, chapter thirteen. He was told to go to Bethel, condemn the idol worship, and return without any diversion. On his way back an old prophet met him and lied to him, saying that an angel had said for him to go home with him. The young prophet was fooled into disobeying God. He never made it home, falling prey to a lion shortly thereafter. He was sincere and he was sincerely wrong. It is not enough to have a sincere heart. Your sincere heart must obey the word of God – not *other than, more than, or less than.*

We must obey God from the heart and from the Bible. We must never begin with our personal reasoning, preferences, or opinions instead of the word of God. When a person makes up their mind as to what he will believe and then turns to the Scriptures, the results are always confusion and contradiction. When a person makes up his mind as to what they believe to be true, and *then* consults the Bible in an effort to find God's agreement, a faulty conclusion is inevitable.

Friends, it just doesn't work that way. We must begin with the word of God and *then* apply what we have learned with a sincere heart. We must obey God from the heart and from the Bible. We cannot go beyond that which is written. "Whoever transgresses and does not abide in the doctrine of Christ does not have God. He who abides in the doctrine of Christ has both the Father and the Son" (2 John 9). We cannot add to or take from that which is written (Deuteronomy 4:2; Revelation 22:18-19). We cannot think more of men than that which is written (1 Corinthians 4:10).

In order to obey the Lord faithfully, we must hear and receive the word of God with the right heart. The Holy Spirit commands us through James' pen, "Therefore lay aside all filthiness and overflow of wickedness, and receive with meekness the implanted word, which is able to save your souls" (James 1:21).

Paul wrote to the Thessalonians, "For this reason we also thank God without ceasing, because when you received the word of God which you heard from us, you welcomed it not as the word of men, but as it is in truth, the word of God, which also effectively works in you who believe" (1 Thessalonians 2:13). We must receive the word of God with this kind of welcoming heart.

In order to obey the gospel faithfully, we must obey the doctrine of Christ from the heart. Paul wrote to the Romans, "But God be thanked that though you were slaves of sin, yet you obeyed from the heart that form of doctrine to which you were delivered. And having been (then, KJV) set free from sin, you became slaves of righteousness" (Romans 6:17-18). When we obey the gospel from the heart and from the Bible, we are set free from sin and become the servants of righteousness.

For a man to serve God faithfully, he must serve Him in sincerity and truth. Joshua admonished the children of Israel to "fear the Lord, (and) serve Him in sincerity and in truth" (Joshua 24:14). Upon confirming Saul as king, Samuel commanded the children of Israel: "Only fear the Lord, and serve Him in truth with all your heart; for consider what great things He has done for you" (1 Samuel 12:24). The Lord must be served in truth with all our heart. Everything we do for God must be done from the heart and from the Bible. Anything *other than, more than, or less than* is disobedience.

If man is to worship God faithfully, he must worship from the heart and from the Bible. Jesus told the Samaritan woman at Jacob's well, "But the hour is coming, and now is, when the true worshipers will worship the Father in spirit and truth; for the Father is seeking such to worship Him. God is Spirit, and those who worship Him must worship in spirit and truth" (John 4:23-24).

What kind of worship is God seeking? Jesus said our worship must be in spirit – from the heart – and in truth – from the Bible. Anything *other than, more than, or less than* that is not true worship.

If we are to treat one another faithfully as brothers and sisters in Christ, we must love one another from the heart and from the Bible. "Since you have purified your souls in obeying the truth through the Spirit in sincere love of the brethren, love one another fervently with a pure heart, having been born again, not of corruptible seed but incorruptible, through the word of God which lives and abides forever..." (1 Peter 1:22-23).

257

We are to love one another "in deed and in truth" (1 John 3:18). "And this is His commandment: that we should believe on the name of His Son Jesus Christ and love one another, as He gave us commandment" (1 John 3:23).

Brotherly love is a commandment from the Bible which must be obeyed with a sincere heart, fervently. "Whoever believes that Jesus is the Christ is born of God, and everyone who loves Him who begot also loves him who is begotten of Him. By this we know that we love the children of God, when we love God and keep His commandments" (1 John 5:1-2). Brotherly love must come from the heart and from the Bible.

Moreover, for man to love God acceptably, his love must be from the heart and from the Bible. The greatest commandment is to "love the Lord your God with all your heart, with all your soul, and with all your mind" (Matthew 22:37).

We are to love the Lord our God with *all* of our heart. But, Jesus also said "If you love Me, keep My commandments" (John 14:15). And, "If you keep My commandments, you will abide in My love, just as I have kept My Father's commandments and abide in His love" (John 15:10).

John writes, "For this is the love of God, that we keep His commandments. And His commandments are not burdensome" (1 John 5:3).

IN CONCLUSION

Let us determine to obey God from the heart and from the Bible. Receive the gospel message with a meek and welcoming spirit. Obey that message as it is revealed in God's holy word. The Bible teaches that we must believe that Jesus is the Christ. If we refuse to believe, we will die in our sins (John 8:24). The Lord also teaches us that we are to repent of our sins. If we refuse to repent we shall perish in those sins (Luke 13:3, 5). We are also taught to be baptized so that we can wash away our sins (Acts 22:16). If we refuse to be baptized, we cannot enter the kingdom of heaven (John 3:3, 5).

When we obey the Bible with a meek and contrite spirit, God saves us and adds us to His church. A person can serve God just as they did in the Bible. Obey God from the heart and from the Bible – nothing other than, more than, or less than that is required of you.

IF I HAD ONLY ONE LAST SERMON TO PREACH

"I charge you therefore before God and the Lord Jesus Christ, who will judge the living and the dead at His appearing and His kingdom: Preach the word! Be ready in season and out of season. Convince, rebuke, exhort, with all long-suffering and teaching. For the time will come when they will not endure sound doctrine, but according to their own desires, because they have itching ears, they will heap up for themselves teachers; and they will turn their ears away from the truth, and be turned aside to fables" (2 Timothy 4:1-4).

Preaching is a great privilege. It is a privilege to serve the Lord in His kingdom in this way. Moreover, it is a great blessing to be a gospel preacher. God has been good to me in granting me this great blessing of being a gospel preacher. I hope that He will continue to use me as He sees fitting. Yet, I know that someday the day will come when I will preach my last sermon, sheath my sword, and travel the pathway unknown to mortal eyes.

Truly, every sermon should be preached as though it is the last sermon for the preacher. And, every sermon should be received as though it is the last sermon by the listener. If I had the ability to know when that last sermon would be, I would want to make sure that the sermon was in the first place true to the word of God. I would want it to be a *gospel* sermon. In second place, I would hope that it would be an edifying sermon to those who heard it. I would determine to exhort and to admonish the listeners about things sacred and eternal. I would want to preach as a dying man to dying people. I would hope to preach as one who was prepared to climb the sunlit slope of Zion, and encourage others to go with me. I would also want to make a few specific points for the sake of a few specific people.

A WORD TO THE LOST

If I had but one last sermon to preach, I would hope that if any dear souls were present that had yet to come in humble obedience to God and His word, that something would be said to impress upon them the severity of their situation and the urgency with which they must act. Yes, if I had only one last sermon to preach, I would want to say a word to the lost. I would want every lost soul to know that there *is* a God in heaven who loves them. He loves us so much that He gave us His only Son to die for our sins.

The sacrifice of God's own Son is without doubt the greatest expression of His love for man. If we will only look to the cross, we will find proof of God's love for every soul. However despised or rejected a person may be, that person is the object of God's love. When one is without a friend, a home, or even a penny to his name, that person is still the object of God's love. No matter how lowly the individual, God loves him. No matter how perilous his life and living may be in this world, God loves him. No matter how wretched a sinner and outcast of society that person may be, God loves him.

Paul tells us that God demonstrated His love to us "in that while we were still sinners, Christ died for us" (Romans 5:8). God sent His Son into a world that was completely given over to wickedness. "All we like sheep have gone astray." John said, "The whole world lies in wickedness" (1 John 5:19). There was "no one righteous, no not one" (Romans 3:10). Just as the world is today, all were sinners and falling short of the glory of God.

God did not hesitate to send His Son to die for us. And, while the cross does not prove to us that we are deserving heirs of such compassion, it certainly proves that "God is love" (1 John 4:8), and that He is truly worthy to be praised. To be heirs of this love is grace divine. We do not deserve it. We have not earned it. And yet, because of the love of God, Deity was clothed in humanity and died as a sin offering so that we might be rescued from hell. Jesus "bore our sins in His own body on the tree, that we, having died to sins, might live for righteousness—by whose stripes you were healed" (1 Peter 2:24).

No other religion is as certain of the love of God as is the Christian religion. In fact, the idea of God's love is at the heart of our religion. This is because of the cross. No other religion has a cross in it. To accept the cross is to accept the love of God and that God is love.

God's love through the cross means even more to us when we come to understand that it was demonstrated to us as we were helpless and could do nothing to reconcile our relationship with Him. "God forbid that I should boast except in the cross of our Lord Jesus Christ, by whom the world has been crucified to me, and I to the world" (Galatians 6:14).

We were as children crying "help" to a father, when we could do no more. No sacrifice we could offer would have been sufficient. No good deed we could have done would have been efficient. We were simply in a helpless and hopeless condition, waiting on the Lord of glory.

It was at this time of utter helplessness that God demonstrated His love, and sent His only begotten Son to reconcile the hopeless world unto Him. And, as ambassadors for Christ we cry out with Paul, "Be ye reconciled to God!"

If I had but one last sermon, I would also want the lost to know how they became lost. One is not born lost. A soul becomes lost because he has sinned against God. Sin brings forth a spiritual death or separation between man and God.

Read with me from James 1:13-15: "Let no one say when he is tempted, 'I am tempted by God'; for God cannot be tempted by evil, nor does He Himself tempt anyone. But each one is tempted when he is drawn away by his own desires and enticed. Then, when desire has conceived, it gives birth to sin; and sin, when it is full-grown, brings forth death." Our sins separate us from God (Isaiah 59:1-2). We must not lie about our sins, hide them, or attempt to justify them. Rather, we should acknowledge them, repent of them, and seek God's forgiveness.

If this was to be the last sermon I would ever preach, I would also want the lost who were listening to know what they must do to receive God's forgiveness. I would want to extend the plan of salvation so clearly and forcefully as to compel them to obey. I would want every lost soul present to know why and how they must hear the gospel. Faith comes by hearing the word of God (Romans 10:17). We must receive this word in a meek and humble spirit (James 1:21).

Every one of us must come to believe that Jesus is the Son of God. Jesus said, "Therefore I said to you that you will die in your sins; for if you do not believe that I am He, you will die in your sins" (John 8:24). If we die in our sins, we cannot be with Him in glory (John 8:21).

We must turn from the sins that have separated us from God. Our sins have caused God to turn His face from us (1 Peter 3:12). We must turn from these sins, and turn toward God. We must confess that Jesus is the Christ. If we choose not to confess Him before men, He will choose not to confess us before His Father (Matthew 10:32-33). We must be born again (John 3:3-5). One is born again by being baptized in water for the forgiveness of sin (Acts 2:38). Upon baptism, souls are raised to live a new life (Romans 6:3-4;

Colossians 2:11-13). Thus, we must live faithfully in that newness of life as a child of God.

A WORD TO THE SAVED

If I had only one last sermon to preach, I would also want to say a word to the saved. I would urge the saved not to forget that there *is* a God in heaven who loves them. Christ loves you so much that He gave Himself for you (Ephesians 5:25-27).

I would also urge you not to forget that you have dedicated your life to serving God. Paul writes, "Do you not know that to whom you present yourselves slaves to obey, you are that one's slaves whom you obey, whether of sin to death, or of obedience to righteousness? But God be thanked that though you were slaves of sin, yet you obeyed from the heart that form of doctrine to which you were delivered. And having been set free from sin, you became slaves of righteousness" (Romans 6:16-18).

The Lord's body must not forget their place in this world. Of you Christ has said, "You are the salt of the earth; but if the salt loses its flavor, how shall it be seasoned? It is then good for nothing but to be thrown out and trampled under foot by men. You are the light of the world. A city that is set on a hill cannot be hidden. Nor do they light a lamp and put it under a basket, but on a lampstand, and it gives light to all who are in the house. Let your light so shine before men, that they may see your good works and glorify your Father in heaven" (Matthew 5:13-16). We have work to do, my brethren!

If I knew I had only one last sermon to preach, I would want to encourage my brethren to finish the course. Paul was looking down the backstretch of life's race when he wrote Timothy saying, "For I am already being poured out as a drink offering, and the time of my departure is at hand. I have fought the good fight, I have finished the race, I have kept the faith. Finally, there is laid up for me the crown of righteousness, which the Lord, the righteous Judge, will give to me on that Day, and not to me only but also to all who have loved His appearing" (2 Timothy 4:6-8).

A WORD TO THE WAYWARD

If I had but one last sermon to preach, and I knew this was it, I would also want to say a word to any wayward Christians who might be listening. I would ask that you consider what you have done. The writer of Hebrews has said you have, "trampled the Son of God underfoot, counted the blood of the covenant by which he was sanctified a common thing, and insulted the Spirit of grace" (Hebrews 10:29).

I would ask that you consider what you have lost. "For if we sin willfully after we have received the knowledge of the truth, there no longer remains a sacrifice for sins, but a certain fearful expectation of judgment, and fiery indignation which will devour the adversaries" (Hebrews 10:26-27).

I would also ask that you consider your fate. "For if, after they have escaped the pollutions of the world through the knowledge of the Lord and Savior Jesus Christ, they are again entangled in them and overcome, the latter end is worse for them than the beginning. For it would have been better for them not to have known the way of righteousness, than having known it, to turn from the holy commandment delivered to them. But it has happened to them according to the true proverb: 'A dog returns to his own vomit,' and, 'a sow, having washed, to her wallowing in the mire'" (2 Peter 2:20-22).

If this was to be my last sermon, I would plead with you to consider what you must do to make things right. Jesus says to the wayward, "Remember therefore from where you have fallen; repent and do the first works..." (Revelation 2:5). Do as the prodigal son. Come to yourself and come home.

Yes, if I had but one last sermon, I would want to repeat Jesus' admonition of endurance for the sake of every brother present: "he who endures to the end shall be saved" (Matthew 24:13); but, "No one, having put his hand to the plow, and looking back, is fit for the kingdom of God" (Luke 9:62).

I would like to encourage every one of you to have the mind of Christ and finish the life and the work God has given you to do. Jesus said to His Father, "I have glorified You on the earth. I have finished the work which You have given Me to do" (John 17:4). Can you say that about yourself?

A WORD TO THE YOUNG

If I had only one last sermon to preach, I would also want to address the youth. I would encourage them to learn to serve the Lord at a young age. "Remember now your Creator in the days of your youth, before the difficult days come, and the years draw near when you say, 'I have no pleasure in them'" (Ecclesiastes 12:1).

Be strong, let the word of God abide in you, and overcome the wicked one (1 John 2:14). Learn from the mistakes and triumphs of others and decide wisely for yourself. Consider Timothy who had a disbelieving father (Acts 16:3), and yet chose to follow the Christian examples of his grandmother and mother (2 Timothy 1:5).

Learn to choose your closest friends wisely. Paul had only Luke to comfort him, at least for a while, in his final, dark, imprisoned hours (2 Timothy 4:10 ff.). How lonely would he have been without Luke? It is important that you have a "Luke" in your life.

I wish young Christians everywhere could know the joy of true brotherly love and Christian fellowship. The best friend you will ever have will be a faithful Christian. The best husband or wife you could ever choose will be a faithful Christian. Loved ones, the best people on earth are faithful Christians.

In a time when we are losing so many of our young, I would exhort them to take care of their souls. The soul is the most precious possession you will ever have. Enthrone Christ in your hearts. Learn to love the Lord with all your heart and might. Take heed to the gospel which you have heard. Be a soul winner. Take responsibility for the health and growth of your home congregation. These are but a few of the things I would say to the young, if I had but one last sermon to preach.

A WORD TO THE AGED

If I had but one last sermon, I would like to say a word to the aged as well. I would encourage them to be examples to their young brethren, children, and acquaintances. It is the sacred place of the older ones to instruct the younger ones. When such counsel is given, young people should listen. Just think of how things might have turned out differently for King Rehoboam had he chosen to listen to the counsel of the older men (1 Kings 12:3 ff.). Had he listened to their wise counsel, he could have become a great king. Instead, he listened to other likeminded young men and divided his country.

The Holy Spirit instructs: "But as for you, speak the things which are proper for sound doctrine: that the older men be sober, reverent, temperate, sound in faith, in love, in patience; the older women likewise, that they be reverent in behavior, not slanderers, not given to much wine, teachers of good things that they admonish the young women to love their husbands, to love their children, to be discreet, chaste, homemakers, good, obedient to their own husbands, that the word of God may not be blasphemed. Likewise exhort the young men to be sober-minded, in all things showing yourself to be a pattern of good works; in doctrine showing integrity, reverence, incorruptibility, sound speech that cannot be condemned, that one who is an opponent may be ashamed, having nothing evil to say of you" (Titus 2:1-8).

If this was my last sermon, I would encourage the older ones to find a young person and teach them to do great things for the Lord. Commit unto them the knowledge you have so that they can teach others also (2 Timothy 2:2). Be a teacher of good things. Teach the young about "the grace of God that brings salvation (and) has appeared to all men, teaching us that, denying ungodliness and worldly lusts, we should live soberly, righteously, and godly in the present age, looking for the blessed hope and glorious appearing of our great God and Savior Jesus Christ, who gave Himself for us, that He might redeem us from every lawless deed and purify for Himself His own special people, zealous for good works" (Titus 2:11-14).

Encourage the young and build them up in the most holy faith. Teach them to live soberly and righteously. Teach them to be zealous for good works. Be willing to have an influence as long as God is willing to use you. "For none of us lives to himself, and no one dies to himself" (Romans 14:7).

Follow the examples of Abraham, Moses, and the beloved apostle John who each served God and exerted a tremendous influence even at an advanced age. Never feel as though you have outlived your usefulness or your influence. Everyone is influencing someone and it is for each person to determine whether that influence will be for the better or for the worse.

I would like to encourage my older brethren to teach our young people that the church is a family. Be a godly role model for them. Help young Christians to secure their hearts. Brethren, be fatherly figures in the gospel as Paul was to Timothy and Titus. Sisters, be as Dorcas who was full of good works and charitable deeds (Acts 9:36). Teach your young sisters in Christ to do likewise and encourage them to live as pure, godly women.

IN CONCLUSION

If I had but one last sermon to preach, I would want to speak to the lost, the saved, the wayward, the young, and the old. These are the people I would hope to address, if I had but one last sermon to preach. With this sermon, I have done my best to give you the very sermon that I would be pleased with preaching, if I knew it was to be my last. I can honestly say that should this indeed be my last sermon, I would be pleased to know that this was it.

Now, I ask that you share with me the decision you would make if you had but one last chance to make it. If you knew this was the last sermon you would ever receive, what would be your reception? I ask that you respond to Him as though you had but one last response to give. What would it be?

About the Author

Andy Erwin (B.A., M.Div., Amridge University) is the minister for the West Fayetteville church of Christ in Fayetteville, Tennessee. He is also the editor of the *Gospel Gleaner* and has authored the following books *Each One Reach One: A Study of Church Growth and Personal Evangelism*; *Select Studies in Restoration History: 1700-Present Day*; and *You've Been A Good Brother, Willie: The Biography and Sermons of W.A. Bradfield*.

In addition to his preaching and writing, Andy Erwin has been an instructor for the Middle Tennessee School of Preaching and Biblical Studies since 2003. He has also participated in six religious debates on a variety of subjects.

Andy and Melanie Erwin have four children: Jackson, Camille, Hannah, and Emma.

If you would like to receive a free subscription for the
Gospel Gleaner write to:
Gospel Gleaner Publications
PO BOX 456
Fayetteville, TN 37334